CAPE EDITIONS 34

General Editor: NATHANIEL TARN

Conversations with Claude Lévi-Strauss

G. CHARBONNIER

Translated by
John and Doreen Weightman

JONATHAN CAPE
THIRTY BEDFORD SQUARE
LONDON

English version first published 1969
by Jonathan Cape Ltd, 30 Bedford Square, London WC1
Reprinted 1970
Translated from the French
Entretiens avec Claude Lévi-Strauss
© 1961 by Librairie Plon et les Éditions René Julliard
Translation © 1969 by Jonathan Cape Ltd

SBN Paperback 224 61666 8
Hardback 224 61665 X

Printed and bound in Great Britain
by Richard Clay (The Chaucer Press), Ltd
Bungay, Suffolk

Contents

*Conversations
with Claude
Lévi-Strauss*

[These conversations were broadcast by the R.T.F. (Radiodiffusion-Télévision Française) during October, November and December 1959.]

I

THE ANTHROPOLOGIST AND THE PUBLIC[1]

GEORGES CHARBONNIER. Claude Lévi-Strauss, for a long time now there has been a great deal of discussion about the divorce between the painter and the spectator, the composer and the listener, the poet and the reader and, more generally, between the artist on the one hand and art-lovers, buyers of pictures, consumers or the merely indifferent, on the other. Would it not be appropriate to point out that there is an even more complete divorce between the scientist and the man in the street?

The gap between the painter and his public can be seen as being no more than the concrete expression of

[1] In England and America, the terms 'ethnology', 'social and cultural anthropology' and 'physical anthropology' respectively cover the historical, sociological and biological aspects of the study of non-literate societies. In France, the term *anthropologie* has usually meant 'physical anthropology' while *ethnologie* covers our 'ethnology' and 'social and cultural anthropology'. Thus, while the terms *anthropologie sociale et culturelle* are gradually coming into general usage in France, the words *ethnologie*, *ethnologue* and *ethnologique* should be translated 'anthropology', 'anthropologist' and 'anthropological'. We have followed this procedure here. In two instances where a slight distinction is introduced in the French text between the usual *ethnologue* and the term *anthropologue*, we have shown this by means of footnotes. (Editor)

a difference in sensibility, whereas the divorce between the scientist and the ordinary man is indica-
tive, in the first place, of a disparity in knowledge and
in the ability to acquire knowledge. It is perhaps in
this disparity that, in our time, the idea of inequality
finds its crudest and cruellest expression. The scientist
is a man who knows, and who knows how to know,
whereas we non-scientists have only our vague reading of our day-to-day experiences to go on. Furthermore, the scientist finds himself with ever more real
power at his disposal. We no longer have much faith
in the power of politicians, but we believe more and
more in that of the scientists. We used to have doubts
about the moral sense of politicians, but that problem
has ceased to interest us. What we have doubts about
now is the scientists' moral conscience. We criticize
the scientist for pursuing research which may lead to
destructive ends. We criticize him for having succeeded in making pure research coincide with the
potential destruction of humanity. In short, for having
ensured the advancement of physics through the creation of the atom bomb. We criticize the physicist for
having found an alibi, an indestructible alibi, in knowledge; for having adopted, as regards knowledge, a
position similar to the alibi of the 'justifiable case' in
the legal world. We all have a shrewd suspicion that
if jurists have invented a theory about the misuse of
the law, this must be because misuse of the law has
existed as long as law itself, and then we ask ourselves
whether this misuse of knowledge might not coincide

with the use of knowledge, or, what is more, with the creation of the body of knowledge.

We demand of the scientist that he should estimate the effects of his acts of knowledge and that he should keep a check on those effects. We ask that, in calculating his powers, he should assume full responsibility for their conscious exercise. But at the same time, we think him incapable of doing so.

For previous instances, we need look no further than the atomic bomb. Are there any instances at the present time and will there be further instances in the future? In short, we feel we are being attacked by knowledge and we are afraid that the conception of man which we cherish, vague though it is, may vanish altogether.

Until now, however, we believed that, in the arts, we had found a refuge beyond the scientists' reach. We thought they were the very abode of freedom, an area in which no law would be formulated nor any be applied. And we poured scorn on professors of aesthetics. We were sure that mathematics would never invade the realm of art to create that special kind of beauty which we insist is human, solely human and beyond mathematical calculation, because it is an article of faith with us average men that the human is that which eludes mathematical calculation. Everything which can be calculated is inhuman; every sphere invaded by mathematics is so much ground wrested from man. This is tantamount to saying that, within our admittedly vague notion of science, we establish a scale of values which is in inverse ratio to the amount of pure mathematics utilized in each branch – if I may express myself in this rough and ready way.

According to this emotional classification, physics constitutes a greater threat than the so-called 'social' sciences. We are strongly prejudiced in favour of pre-history, archaeology and anthropology. We have long known – since anthropologists themselves have made the point clear to us – that their way of studying man involves a poetic approach to the subject. If art, and the artist's approach, can, in certain cases, be connected with scientific methods, we are in a hurry to take this as a justification of our habitual way of thinking and as a means of safe-guarding our conception of man.

However, we now understand that anthropology aims solely at exactness and on occasion abandons poetic truth to the object in favour of accuracy, and we have an unmistakable feeling that the ground is giving way beneath us. Yet we want at all costs to be reassured.

However obvious this may be, we want to be assured that the scientist is a man like us, that in everyday affairs he allows himself to be guided by his emotions and does not rationalize his life entirely. For instance, whereas the scientist talks of political economy and 'sociology', we use the looser term 'politics'. We are involved in an area of action which we refer to as 'political'. We find ourselves making decisions, or imagine we are making them, and for us, this is tantamount to the same thing. And yet we believe – we cling stubbornly to the hope – that you scientists will inevitably be drawn into the political field. And when you enter this field, do you do so as scientists or does emotion reassert itself? Do you become similar to someone like myself?

CLAUDE LÉVI-STRAUSS. I would not like to put you into a position in which I might feel compelled to …

G.C. I am putting myself into the worst possible position … deliberately.

C.L.-S. Then so will I. Naturally, I have political convictions like everybody else. It is impossible for me not to have political convictions since I am forced to do so by public pressure and since my political conscience is daily roused by the spectacle of so much stupidity and wickedness. But my political attitude has not really been modified by the fact that I became an anthropologist: it remains outside, and almost impervious to, my professional thinking and so I must admit that it is an essentially emotional attitude. This is all the more true in that it is very difficult to bridge the gap between the objective attitude one strives to maintain when considering other communities from the outside and the situation in which one finds oneself, willy-nilly, inside one's own society.

G.C. Without asking you to go into specific details and quote concrete instances, may I inquire if, as a scientist, you ever put your finger on certain discrepancies? Do you ever think: 'I am led to the conclusion that such and such is probably true, yet I react exactly as if it were not true … '?

C.L.-S. Certainly, when I try to analyse my own society in the light of information I have about other societies that I study with sympathetic understanding and almost with affection, I am struck by certain contradictions; when I witness certain decisions or certain modes of behaviour in my own society, I am filled with indignation and disgust, whereas if I observe similar, or relatively comparable, ones in so-called primitive societies, I make no attempt at a value judgment. I try to understand why things are as they are and I even work on the assumption that since these modes of action and attitudes exist, there must be some reason behind them.

G.C. Yes, even though I am not an anthropologist, I have been struck by this in reading your books, that is your anthropological works. I don't remember which primitive society you were dealing with, but the precise reference is not important. The general impression was that cannibalism and torture were, in a sense, justifiable. When the reasons for a given phenomenon are understood, the phenomenon itself is justified. I don't mean that you justify it – what I mean is that, as a reader, I get the impression that the phenomenon is a subject for study – and just as fascinating or more fascinating than any other, and that suffering, as a value, has disappeared.

C.L.-S. I would almost go so far as to say that that is how things should be; in fact they never are. We are all specialists to a greater or lesser degree, since we cannot claim to be conversant with the three or four thousand different societies which were still extant towards the end of the nineteenth century – the number must be smaller now, because many have disappeared. It follows that we are forced to choose, and we do so for reasons which are not strictly scientific. In the first place, our choice is dictated by chance, because the circumstances of our careers prompted us to commit ourselves in some particular direction, and then by reasons dependent on personal affinities or antipathies.

I remember that during the last months of his life, my famous American colleague, Robert Lowie – I take him as an example because there are no books more objective, detached and serene than his; as we read them, we get the impression that he is a wholly disinterested scholar who studies these societies with complete objectivity without allowing the slightest personal factor to intrude – told me that he had never felt completely at ease in some of the societies he had studied very thoroughly, and that, in fact, he did not believe he had fully understood them. He explained, for instance, that while he had a whole-hearted affection for the Crow Indians, who live on the plains and wear feather head-dresses – that is, the kind of Indians who are so popular with our children – he hadn't at all the same feelings for the Hopi Indians belonging to the *Pueblos* of the south-western states of America and on whom he had written some excellent studies.

And when I asked him why, he replied, 'I don't really know; but if a Crow Indian punishes his unfaithful wife by cutting off her nose, I can understand his reaction, which in a sense strikes me as being normal. On the other hand, a Hopi Indian, in the same situation, starts praying to ask the gods to withhold rain so that famine afflicts the whole community: this seems to me to be an incomprehensible and almost monstrous attitude which makes my hair stand on end.'

I repeat that, nevertheless, Lowie had done remarkable, even outstanding, research work among both the Crow and the Hopi Indians; but he hadn't the same attitude towards the two groups, since with one of them he was required to make an additional effort. All anthropologists have experiences of this kind.

I cannot deny that when I read descriptions of certain tortures carried out by Mexican Indians or by the Plains Indians of the United States, I am rather revolted. But this feeling cannot in any sense be compared with the infinite horror and scorn which comparable practices in our own society inspire in me. Whereas, with the Indian communities, I try first of all to understand the system of attitudes, beliefs and collective representations within which practices such as these can exist.

G.C. It seems to me that anthropologists are particularly lucky – what I mean by luck is perhaps a deliberate decision on their part – it seems to me that you anthropologists do not stand in the same relationship to your passions as the physicists to theirs; it would seem that you are more successful in coming to terms with your emotions and are able to integrate them more fully into your method of working – not perhaps into the object of your research, but into your method of working. The fact of being an anthropologist,[1] of being interested in human communities and in a certain kind of human being, implies and presupposes a choice.

c.l.-s. It has often been said – I don't know if it is universally true but it is probably true for many of us – that the reason why we took up anthropology was that we had difficulty in adapting ourselves to the social milieu into which we were born.

g.c. That is not quite what I meant. I fully realize that there must be some element of truth in it, and that the anthropologist must have some reason for *going away*, but it seems to me that anthropological research allows him fully to accommodate within himself both the man and the scientist.

c.l.-s. In other words, it teaches us the rather harsh and painful intellectual lesson that we must abandon the conception of a 'Euclidean' sociology – if I may use this expression – just as physicists and astronomers

---

[1] 'Le fait d'être anthropologue, d'être ethnologue, ... '

have taught us that we must no longer believe that all phenomena, from the infinitely small to the infinitely great, occur within a homogeneous form of space. When you study different societies it may be necessary to change your system of reference, and that involves somewhat painful mental gymnastics which furthermore can only be learnt from experience in the field. It is inconceivable, even impossible, to be an armchair anthropologist. I would almost go so far as to say that the effort involved is physical, physically exhausting, and to this extent we can perhaps, if not solve the difficulty to which you alluded, at least understand that it is insoluble, that there are contradictions we must get used to and learn to live with on terms of resigned familiarity.

But that does not make us so very different from the physicist, who also realizes that he cannot carry his analysis beyond a certain degree of refinement because, if he does, he relinquishes the possibility of knowing certain aspects of reality in order to grasp others, these different aspects being complementary to each other. The anthropologist finds himself in a very similar situation. We cannot, at one and the same time, bring our minds to bear both on very different societies and on the one in which we live. When we consider our own society, we use a system of values and a system of references which we have to abandon if we wish to reflect on other societies. And when our readers or listeners say to us: 'But you should be able to compare the two things; you ought to be able to put forward a system of reference which would be valid for both', we perhaps have a slight advantage in that we have grown used to doing without such a system of reference.

G.C. It also seemed to me that the anthropologist who travels far afield and goes to a particular place, which he has to a certain extent chosen, will be applying his methods of investigation to something which, on a concrete level, is equivalent to his own personal 'poetry'.

C.L.-S. Yes, but here we are falling back into …

G.C. It doesn't seem to me that the physicist is quite in this position.

C.L.-S. Why shouldn't he be? If you were to ask two specialists why one of them is a biologist and the other a mathematician, are you sure you would not find that the biologist had a liking for living matter and a curiosity about it, which were deeply rooted in his personal history, whereas the mathematician had different, but no less profoundly motivated, attitudes?

G.C. These would be emotional reasons?

C.L.-S. They would include emotion.

G.C. 'My particular "poetry" exists, *a priori*, in a sense, and I go in a certain direction in order to find it embodied in a concrete form.' Can I say this?

C.L.-S. I may be mistaken, but at first glance, I see no reason why the situation should be different for them from what it is for us.

II

'PRIMITIVE' PEOPLES AND 'CIVILIZED' PEOPLES

GEORGES CHARBONNIER. Claude Lévi-Strauss the scientist has to be very patient with us, for we insist on his answering our questions and it stands to reason that the scientist does not ask questions in the same way as we do. He asks questions in order to acquire knowledge; we ask questions in the interests of self-preservation, in order to preserve that concept of man which we cling to stubbornly, although, as we are well aware, we are unable to define it exactly. We feel an affinity with the anthropologist in so far as he is the kind of scientist who uses his poetic sensibility as a means of acquiring knowledge. We therefore ask him, although that is not his object, to interpret the society in which we live poetically, whereas he, with the precision of an astronomer – I am repeating your own terminology – studies one exceptional kind of social material, a kind of social material which is in a crystalline state, and is distant and remote.

We do not feel that the sociologist represents us, and for a very simple reason: he is able, by a series of mathematical calculations, to forecast the average behaviour of our social groups, and we immediately fear for our freedom. So it is to the anthropologist first and foremost that we want to put the following question: what are the basic functional and structural differences that you observe between the societies which you study and the society in which we live?

CLAUDE LÉVI-STRAUSS. You are asking me the most difficult of all the questions to which the anthropologist is sometimes called upon to reply. It is so difficult that I hardly think a reply is possible. It might well be that this question represents the absolute limit of our knowledge. Before trying to reply to it, it might be as well to ask ourselves why it is so very difficult.

It seems to me that this question masks another, which is whether or not we can set out all human societies on a scale according to a concept of progress, some being more 'primitive' – a term we have to adopt since it is in common usage – and the others what one might call 'more civilized'.

G.C. That is, in fact, one of the questions that I intended to raise by implication, and there are others too.

C.L.-S. Yes, but if you don't mind, let us begin by approaching it from this angle. It seems to me that the great difficulty springs from the fact that it is one thing to look at a society from the outside and quite another to look at it from the inside. When we look at it from the outside, we can put a certain number of positive or negative signs against it, determine the degree of its technical development, the extent of its material production, the size of its population and so on, and coolly give it an objective rating, which we can then compare with the ratings we have given to various other societies.

But when seen from the inside, these few inadequate elements are amplified and transformed for each member of a given society, whatever may be its nature; whether it is the most highly civilized or the most primitive is of no importance, it is bound to be full of subtle significances.

To take an example from a different context, imagine how the death of a given person affects his 'acquaintances' and the members of his family. Seen from the outside, any death is a fairly commonplace event, but for the relatives of the deceased, it represents an upheaval of their whole world. We shall never understand exactly what a bereavement means to a family, if that family is not our own, and when it is not we ourselves who are bereaved.

This kind of difficulty is reminiscent to some extent of the complementarity that the physicists talk about.

It is impossible to determine, at one and the same time, the trajectory and the position of a particle. Similarly, we perhaps cannot both try to get to know a society from the inside and classify it from the outside in relation to other societies. That is the difficulty.

G.C. But that is the general difficulty of anthropology and also of all methods of human investigation.

C.L.-S. This is indeed the difficulty faced by all methods, and I am only trying to explain its particular incidence in anthropology. I was anxious to do so from the outset, but not of course in order to avoid answering your question, to which I must try to reply because it is a question we all ask ourselves and because we cannot help establishing comparisons between societies as different from each other as, say, that of the Australian aborigines, in which pottery, weaving, farming and domestic animals are unknown, and our own society, with its mechanization, thermal energy, electrical energy and now nuclear energy. The difference between such societies is strikingly obvious, and it is impossible for us not to try to understand the reasons for it.

G.C. There is, in current use, a whole vocabulary, the underlying significance of which ought to be laid bare, since we are men of this day and age living inside large communities, and even when we try, in spite of our lack of scientific training, to adopt an impartial position, we nevertheless feel that the word 'large' means something.

C.L.-S. Objectively, contemporary societies and those communities which we call 'primitive' are not in the same category as regards size. This is an observable fact, and if you don't mind, I would like to make it my starting-point. We can see our civilization as a very complex combination. The difference in size can, broadly speaking, be likened to the difference between compound molecules, which are made up of a combination of several thousand atoms, and simple molecules, which contain only a small number. The difference is twofold: it relates both to size and complexity of organization. How is the difference to be explained in the instance we are concerned with here?

I am going to put forward an initial hypothesis: in doing so, I confess that I am playing the devil's advocate, since I will not bide by it, but it seems to me that we should begin by considering it as a possibility.

Suppose an inveterate roulette player sets out not only to pick the lucky number, but to work out a very complex combination dependent on, say, ten or a hundred previous spins of the wheel, and determined by certain rules regarding the alternation of red and black, or even and odd numbers. This complex combination might be achieved right away, or at the thousandth or millionth attempt or never at all. Yet it would never occur to us to say that, had he accomplished his combination only at the seven hundred and twenty-fifth attempt, all the previous attempts were indispensable to his success. He was successful at that particular moment, but the moment might well have come later, and that was only how things turned out; yet during the initial attempts there was no progress which might have been considered as the necessary pre-condition of his success. And I might use the analogy in order to reply to the question you put to me a short while ago. Let us say, then, that it was necessary to wait a few hundred thousand years before that most complex combination – western civilization – came into being. Mankind might have achieved the combination at an early stage, or might have done so very much later, but the fact is that it has achieved it at this particular moment, and there is no reason why this should be so, it just is. However, you may say: 'That is not very satisfactory.'

G.C. No, it does not strike me as being satisfactory. As a non-specialist, I look upon the time factor as being important.

C.L.-S. I would agree with you, but let us try to define the time factor more closely. What does it consist of? I believe that here we must refer to an essential acquisition of culture, which was the pre-condition of that totalization of knowledge and utilization of past experience that we feel, more or less intuitively, to have been the source of our civilization. The cultural acquisition, the conquest, to which I am referring, is writing.

It is certain that a people can only take advantage of previous acquisitions in so far as these have been made permanent in writing. I know, of course, that the societies we call primitive often have a quite staggering capacity for remembering, and we have been told about Polynesian communities who can recite straight off family trees involving dozens of generations; but that kind of feat obviously has its limits. Writing had to be invented so that the knowledge, the experiments, the happy or unhappy experiences of each generation could accumulate, so that, working on the basis of this capital, succeeding generations would be able not only to repeat the same endeavours, but also turn all previous ones to good account in order to improve techniques and achieve fresh progress. Do you agree on this point?

G.C. I think so. I don't see that it is at all debatable.

C.L.-S. Here, then, we have something we can hold on to, since the invention of writing took place in time and space. We know that it occurred in the Eastern Mediterranean some three or four thousand years before the birth of Christ, and that it was a vital discovery.

G.C. But is there something exceptional about the emergence of a phenomenon such as the invention of writing at one particular time and in one particular place? As a non-specialist, I ask – why there?

C.L.-S. Why there? I may seem to be contradicting what I was suggesting a moment ago, but I feel that at this point we should introduce a new idea. Writing appeared in the history of humanity some three or four thousand years before the beginning of our era, at a time when humanity had already made its most essential and fundamental discoveries; it appeared not before, but immediately after, what is called the 'neolithic revolution' – the discovery of those civilized skills which still form the basis of our lives: agriculture, the domestication of animals, pottery-making,

27

weaving – a whole range of processes which were to allow human beings to stop living from day to day as they had done in paleolithic times, when they depended on hunting or on the gathering of fruit, and to accumulate ...

G.C. ... to build up a reserve stock.

C.L.-S. Yes, precisely, to have a reserve stock. Now, we should be wrong to think that discoveries as vital as these materialized all at once, and purely as the result of chance. Agriculture, to take only one example, represents a mass of knowledge, the accumulated experience of many generations which was handed down from one to the other before it became something which could be turned to effective account. It has often been pointed out that domestic animals are not just wild species which have become domesticated; they are wild species which have been completely transformed by man, and this transformation, which was the necessary pre-condition of man's ability to use them, must have occupied long periods of time and called for great persistence and prolonged and concentrated experimentation. Now all that was possible without the existence of writing.

Therefore, although writing seemed to us a moment ago to be a pre-condition of progress, we must never lose sight of the fact that certain essential forms of progress, perhaps the most essential ever achieved by humanity, were accomplished without the help of writing.

G.C. But we are inevitably led to ask ourselves the same question with regard to each of these instances of progress. As non-scientists, we wonder why a particular kind of progress occurred in a particular place, And the farther back in time I go, the more frequently the question arises.

C.L.-S. The problem is not quite the same in connection with the neolithic era.

G.C. But the question still remains: what are the underlying conditions of any instance of progress?

C.L.-S. Yes, but it is by no means certain that the major conquests of the neolithic age occurred in one place and at one moment in time. It is even likely that in certain conditions – and some attempt has been made to define them: the relative isolation of human communities living in narrow mountain valleys with the advantage of natural irrigation, and protected by their isolated situation from invasion by foreign populations – the discoveries of the neolithic age occurred independently in different regions of the world. Whereas, as far as writing is concerned, the situation would appear to be much clearer: the appearance of writing in our civilization is at least quite definitely localized. And so we must ask ourselves with what other phenomena it is linked. What was happening at the same time as the invention of writing? What accompanied it? What may have conditioned it? In this connection, there is one fact which can be established: the only phenomena which, always and in all parts of the world, seems to be linked with the appearance of writing, and not only in the eastern Mediterranean but also in China in the earliest known period, and even in those regions of America where crude attempts at writing had occurred before the conquest, is the establishment of hierarchical societies, consisting of masters and slaves, and where one part of the population is made to work for the other part.

And when we consider the first uses to which writing was put, it would seem quite clear that it was connected first and foremost with power : it was used for inventories, catalogues, censuses, laws and instructions; in all instances, whether the aim was to keep a check on material possessions or on human beings, it is evidence of the power exercised by some men over other men and over worldly possessions.

G.C. Social control of power.

C.L.-S. A check on power and at the same time the means by which power was regulated. We have followed a somewhat tortuous route; starting from the problem of progress, we saw that it was connected with the capitalization or totalization of knowledge. This process itself only appeared possible after the point at which writing came into existence, and writing itself, in the first instance, seemed to be associated in any permanent way only with societies which were based on the exploitation of man by man. Therefore, the problem of progress becomes more complicated and appears two-dimensional, instead of uni-dimensional; for if, in order to establish his ascendancy over nature, man had to subjugate man and treat one section of mankind as an object, we can no longer give a simple and unequivocal answer to the questions raised by the concept of progress.

III

CLOCKS AND STEAM-ENGINES

GEORGES CHARBONNIER. Claude Lévi-Strauss, today I would like to ask you to develop the comparison between primitive societies and modern societies. I am returning to the question I put to you during the last broadcast in order to elucidate those points which, in the last analysis, make the two kinds of society so profoundly different from each other.

CLAUDE LÉVI-STRAUSS. Let me go back, then, to your initial question : what is the fundamental difference between them. I believe we must start from the concept (which can, incidentally, be embodied in an extremely wide variety of concrete forms) of societies founded on the exploitation of one section of the social body by another section, or else societies – I apologize for using modern terms which have very little meaning in this context – which are democratic in character and which we refer to as primitive. In short, societies are rather like machines, and it is a well known fact that there are two main types of machine : mechanical machines and thermodynamic machines. The former are those which use the energy with which they were supplied at the outset and which, in theory, could go on operating indefinitely with this energy, provided they were very well constructed and were not subject to friction and heating. Thermodynamic machines, on the other hand, such as the steam-engine, operate on the basis of a difference in temperature between their component parts, between the boiler and the condenser; they can do a tremendous amount of work, far more than the others, but in the process they use up and destroy their energy.

I would say that, in comparison with our own great society, with all the great modern societies, the societies studied by the anthropologist are in a sense 'cold' societies rather than 'hot' societies, or like clocks in relation to steam-engines. They are societies which create the minimum of that disorder which the physicists call 'entropy', and they tend to remain indefinitely in their initial state, and this explains why they appear to us as static societies with no history.

Our modern societies are not only societies which make extensive use of the steam-engine; structurally, they resemble the steam-engine in that they work on the basis of a difference in potential, which finds concrete expression in different forms of social hierarchy. Whether we call it slavery, serfdom or class distinction is not of any fundamental importance, if we stand back and take a broad, panoramic view of the situation. Societies like these have managed to produce within themselves a kind of disequilibrium which they use to create, at one and the same time, much more order – we have mechanized societies – and greater disorder, greater entropy, on the level of human relations.

G.C. The immediate question is: how is the individual affected by this disequilibrium that the collectivity uses, and what is the true significance of the word 'inequality' in a primitive society, as opposed to a contemporary society?

C.L.-S. There is quite a considerable difference. I am anxious not to generalize, because if I tried to express the difference in fairly broad terms, exceptions could be quoted. Of course, behind what we call 'primitive societies' there are all kinds of social organizations, and it would be impossible for me to over-emphasize the fact that there can be just as great a difference between two primitive societies as between either of them and our own society.

There have been primitive societies with a caste-system. India, which is not a 'primitive' society since it had a form of writing, is certainly not the only society of this type. But nevertheless, the main, over-all difference is that primitive societies try, either consciously or unconsciously, to avoid that division between the various members of the community which made possible, or encouraged, the development of Western civilization. And it seems to me that one of the most convincing proofs of this can be found in their political organization. There are many primitive societies – I will not claim that this is true of them all, but such societies can be found all over the world in a

34

great variety of regions – in which we can discern the beginnings of political organization and of popular or representative government, since decisions are taken by the whole of the community which meets together to hold council, or by outstanding persons, such as heads of clans, priests or religious leaders. In societies like these, people consult together and vote. But issues are only settled by unanimous decision. It seems to be believed that if, at the time of making an important decision, there existed, even in the tiniest fraction of the society, feelings of bitterness such as are normally associated with being the loser in an election, resentment and disappointment at not having been supported would produce a powerful and almost magical effect and jeopardize the result that had been obtained.

This, moreover, is the reason why in certain societies – I am thinking of examples in the South Sea Islands – when an important decision has to be taken, a kind of ritual combat is organized a day or two days before, so that all old quarrels are liquidated in fights which are to all intents and purposes simulated, but in which there are sometimes a few casualties, in spite of attempts to minimize the risks. In this way, the society starts off by removing all grounds for dissension, and it is only when this has been done that the refreshed and rejuvenated community, having rid itself of all differences of opinion, is in a position to take a decision which will be unanimous, and thus express the united will of the whole community.

G.C. In other words, if I have understood rightly, there

is a state of unanimity which is independent of the decision. A state of unanimity is created and is then brought to bear on the decision to be taken.

C.L.-S. That's right. A state of unanimity is thought to be indispensable so that the group can go on existing as a group. That is, if you would agree to take into consideration what we were saying a moment ago, the process is an insurance against the risk of division, against the danger that a form of social hierarchy might be surreptitiously created within the group, thus causing a rift between those on the right side and those on the wrong side. In other words, there must be no minority; the society tries to go on functioning like a clock in which all the parts of the mechanism work together harmoniously, and not like those machines which seem to conceal a latent antagonism at the very centre of their mechanism – the antagonism between the source of heat and the cooling device.

G.C. I seem to detect an echo of Rousseau's ideas in what you are saying?

C.L.-S. Why not?

G.C. Unanimity, as defined by Jean-Jacques Rousseau, consists in the unanimous decision to respect the decision taken by the majority. This unanimity is very like the unanimity you have been defining.

C.L.-S Of course. Rousseau knew nothing about the

examples I have just quoted, because problems relating to the political life of primitive peoples began to be studied only comparatively recently, and in Rousseau's day there was not enough data available. Nevertheless, Rousseau saw very clearly that an act of unanimity is the theoretical pre-condition of the existence of a society; this is a principle that very humble communities have applied systematically. In Rousseau's case, the main difficulty occurs when he tries to make transition from the rule of unanimity, which is the only legally justifiable rule, to the practice of election by absolute majority.

G.C. Rousseau thinks of unanimity as being accepted: I renounce my freedom in order to have a share in the general sovereignty.

C.L.-S. Of course, the general will is not, in Rousseau's view, the will of the whole, or of the majority of the population, expressed on particular occasions; it is the latent and continuous decision whereby each individual agrees to exist as a member of a group.

G.C. Precisely. We are not unanimous in taking the decision; we are unanimous in obeying the decision which has been taken. It seems to me that this is quite close to the state you have just defined.

C.L.-S. I entirely agree with you. I believe that in *The Social Contract* – since this is the work we have in mind at the moment – Rousseau formulated the most profound idea, and the one which most readily admits of generalization – that is, can be verified in relation to a very large number of societies – about political organization, and even about the theoretical conditions of any possible political organization.

G.C. However, we are a long way from social structures such as we know them. And, reflecting on what you said a little while ago about our kind of society, which can only function on the basis of a difference in potential, I am forced to conclude that democracy is absolutely impossible in our social state. If the difference is indispensable for the running of the machine, if society is obliged to maintain the difference in order to survive, it follows that any form of democracy is impossible.

C.L.-S. Here you are leading me off into a field which is not quite that of the anthropologist, since you are asking me to base my argument not on the little clocks to which I compared primitive societies a moment ago, but on the huge steam-engines that our contemporary societies resemble. However, I believe that, without carrying the discussion to a final conclusion, we might try to pursue the argument a little further along the lines already indicated.

What I was saying can be summed up as follows: the societies we refer to as primitive can, up to a point, be considered as systems where entropy is unknown or exists only in a very weak form, and which function at a temperature of absolute zero – not zero as understood by the physicist, but in the 'historical' sense : this is what we mean when we say that these societies have no history – and consequently they are characterized to a very high degree by phenomena of a mechanical nature, which in their case are more important than statistical phenomena. It is most striking that the kind of data with which anthropologists feel most at home, such as the laws of kinship and marriage, economic exchanges, rites and myths, can often be compared to small-scale mechanisms, which operate with extreme regularity and complete certain cycles, the machine passing through a succession of states before returning to its starting point, and beginning its rotations all over again.

Societies like our own, which have a history, operate, I would say, at a higher temperature or, to be more exact, there are greater differentials between the internal temperatures of the system, differentials which are caused by social differences.

We should not, then, draw a distinction between 'societies with no history' and 'societies which have histories'. In fact, every human society has a history, and they all go equally far back, since all history dates from the birth of mankind. But whereas so-called primitive societies are surrounded by the substance of history and try to remain impervious to it, modern societies interiorize history, as it were, and turn it into the motive power of their development.

And now I return to the question you asked me at the beginning, namely, how far is the difference in potential inevitable ?

In actual fact, both aspects are inherent in every society. A society is at once a machine and the work done by that machine. As a steam-engine, it produces entropy, but if we look upon it as a mechanism, it produces order. This dual aspect – order and disorder – corresponds, in the language of anthropology, to two ways of looking at any civilization: there is, on the one hand, culture, and on the other, society. By culture, we mean the relationships that the members of a given civilization have with the external world, and by society, we mean more especially the relations men have with each other. Culture produces organization: ploughing the land, building houses, manufacturing objects, etc. ...

G.C. It follows, then, that society is divorced from the world.

C.L.-S. That is so, yet it continues to have a relationship of complementarity with the world. It is nevertheless striking that Gobineau – who was the first person to perceive the presence of entropy, that disorder which is a concomitant factor of progress and an essential feature of society – should have located it 'naturally', as it were, as far away as possible from culture, and farther away than he ought to have done; he placed it in nature, at the level of racial differences. He had, then, a clear grasp of the contrast but, having been the first to notice it, he over-estimated its extent.

This being the case, we might say that any social field – if we call a society a social field – produces entropy, or disorder, as a society, and creates order, as a culture. It is this inverse relationship which, in my view, expresses the difference between the peoples we call primitive and those we call civilized.

Primitive peoples produce very little order by means of their culture. Nowadays, we call them the under-developed peoples. But they produce very little entropy in their societies. On the whole, these societies are egalitarian, mechanical in type, and governed by the law of unanimity to which we referred a moment ago. The civilized peoples, on the other hand, produce a great deal of order in their culture, as is shown by mechanization and by the great achievements of civilization, but they also produce a great deal of entropy in their societies, in the form of social conflicts and political struggles, which, as we saw, are the things that primitive peoples guard against, perhaps more consciously and systematically than we might have supposed.

The great problem of civilization has, therefore, been to maintain differentials. We have seen these ensured by means of slavery, then serfdom, and lastly with the creation of a proletariat.

But as the working-class struggle tends, to some extent, to iron out the differences, our society has had to look for fresh ways of establishing differentials – colonialism and the so-called imperialist policies, for instance – that is, it has had constantly to try, either within the society itself or by subjecting conquered peoples, to create a differential between a ruling section and a section that is ruled; but such a differential is always provisional, as it is in a steam-engine which tends towards immobility because the temperature of the cold element rises while that of the hot element falls.

Differentials tend, therefore, to even themselves out, and each time it has been necessary to create new ones. When this became too difficult within the social group, more complex schemes were put into effect, and the colonial empires can be quoted as an example.

You were asking me whether this is inevitable and irreversible. It is conceivable that, for modern societies, progress and the achievement of a great degree of social justice might depend on transferring entropy from society to culture. This may seem a very abstract way of putting it, yet I am only repeating Saint-Simon's statement that the problem of modern times is how to effect the transition from the governing of men to the administration of things. 'Government of men' corresponds to society and increasing entropy; 'administration of things' corresponds to culture and the creation of an increasingly varied and complex order.

Nevertheless, there will always be a disparity, almost a direct contrast, between the just societies of the future and the societies studied by the anthropologist. All of them might be said to function at a temperature very close to zero, in the historical sense, but the former on the level of society, and the latter on the level of culture. This is what we are expressing or perceiving, in a vague way, when we say that industrial civilization has a dehumanizing effect.

IV

LEVELS OF AUTHENTICITY

GEORGES CHARBONNIER. If I have understood you rightly, within a primitive society there can be no break between the different elements of the population. I realize that there may well be differences in wealth, but the kind of inequality which prevails in a primitive society is not the same as in our societies.

CLAUDE LÉVI-STRAUSS. Let us say that this is true at least in those societies which provide the best examples, because, I repeat, there are societies which cannot easily be fitted into one particular classification. They may belong to one category in so far as they have no form of writing, and yet show the beginnings of economic exploitation. I am thinking of certain native societies along the Canadian coast of the Pacific, the ones we are so familiar with because of their huge, superbly carved totem poles. These societies practised slavery, and it is undeniable that one class accumulated wealth at the expense of another. So we must proceed cautiously and establish contrasts only between the extreme forms of each type of society.

G.C. Does there not exist in Western societies a kind

of differential which it is particularly difficult to imagine existing in a primitive society? Are there not divisions within the group which do not correspond to any particular difference or class distinction on the economic level?

C.L.-S. What exactly do you mean?

G.C. I get the impression that in some large countries, such as the United States or France, there is almost what one might call a gulf between that part of the group which devotes its energies to production and the part which is dedicated to the genuine development of culture. Is this differential a result of our social structure? Will there never be any means of bridging it? Is it indispensable for the functioning of Western societies? I get the impression of a lack of harmony, a kind of discordance, which is an observable phenomenon. I took the United States and France as examples, but I imagine that the same phenomenon is visible in other countries. The United States and France spring to mind, because these are the two countries where I seem to see it in its most characteristic form. It is as if consciousness had become the prerogative of a limited number of individuals and all the others were totally devoid of it, or – to put the point still more bluntly – as if consciousness had taken refuge inside a minority, while knowledge eluded certain people because it was too remote and too complex; but perhaps this is too simple a way of looking at things.

C.L.-S. What you are referring to is specialization rather than the establishment of a hierarchy, and I think that we could find examples of both in native societies. But it is undoubtedly true that they are societies in which the whole of the population participates much more fully and completely in the group culture than is the case in Western societies.

G.C. I have a very clear impression that our own social group, taken as a whole – we could consider others too : I am not implying that France is the only example – does not identify itself with those individuals who secrete or develop its culture.

C.L.-S. Yes, I see what you mean, and my reply would be that both possibilities may occur in practice. In the societies we call primitive, we observe a collective participation in culture, in the form of elaborate religious ceremonies, feasts or dances which occupy a considerable place in the life of the community – as great, and sometimes an even greater place, than those activities connected with production. It follows that the sages, priests and ceremonial leaders are the embodiment and exemplification of a mode of life, a pattern of behaviour and a way of understanding the universe, which are characteristic of the group as a whole, and this is clearly the exact opposite of the situation you describe in Western societies. But let us consider other instances, for example the blacksmith caste in African societies, or in certain other societies of the pastoral type : blacksmiths are connected, not with animal and vegetable life, but with metal – ore which is found underground – and with fire; they are the custodians of knowledge and technical skills which are of a different order from those known to the group. Consequently, they are assigned a special position, and are looked upon with a mixture of respect and fear, admiration and hostility, and this, I think, resembles, or tends to resemble, the position assigned to certain specialists in contemporary society.

G.C. But is there a general desire to be rid of them, or is the necessity for their presence completely accepted?

C.L.-S. Oh, feelings are very mixed. I was particularly struck on reading a newspaper account – I didn't see the original text – of the results of a recent inquiry carried out in the U.S.A. among young people of both sexes, to find out exactly what kind of mental picture adolescents have of the 'scientist' (and, of course, nowadays 'scientist' means 'atomic physicist'). I got the impression that this mental picture and the corresponding attitudes involved a mixture of fear and repulsion (the girls declared that they would never marry a scientist), together with an almost mystical and religious admiration. Such attitudes are very similar to those which can be observed in primitive societies with regard to the blacksmith caste.

G.C. I hope you will pardon my impoliteness in quoting the following remark from Gobineau. I was very forcibly struck by the fact that in one of his short stories, he makes a character say (in speaking of another): 'Il avait une sale petite gueule de savant.'[1] This remark seems to me to be very symptomatic. Gobineau uses the word *savant*, but it seems to me that we are to take it to mean not only 'scientist' but also 'all those who secrete a mode of thought' – that is, artists, poets, writers, in short all those people who are referred to as 'intellectuals'. I seem to notice that, in Western societies, these people are becoming more and more cut off from the rest of the community. They secrete culture, but the group does not consider that its culture is being evolved by this minority. It seems to me that the minority is rejected by the group, and that the break between the group and the intellectuals within it is far more important and far more irremediable than any differences of an economic nature between social classes, because such differences tend perhaps to even themselves out.

C.L.-S. It is undoubtedly quite a different kind of break.

G.C. Is the particular break we are referring to a result of our social structure? Is it a necessary condition for the functioning of our society?

C.L.-S. At this point, I must apologize and plead incompetence: I cannot answer your question, because all problems relating to the role, or the place, of the

[1] 'He had the scientist's typically ugly little mug.' The French word *savant* means both scientist and scholar.

artist in those societies we refer to as primitive, and it is clear that you yourself are thinking much more of the artist ...

G.C. Oh no, not at all.

C.L.-S. But you must admit that there is a big difference, because a scientist, a good scientist, is practically certain to be able to make a career for himself.

G.C. But the artist, too, can have a career. He too can have a place in society. Even Baudelaire had a place.

C.L.-S. Not quite; and not in his own lifetime.

G.C. I think that more artists find a place in society than is generally admitted.

C.L.-S. You are asking me to make a comparison, but I would not be an anthropologist if I did not abstain from commenting on the position of one particular society, which happens to be our own, in the light of observations deriving from other societies.

Moreover, we know very little about the nature of the artist, or of the people who might be referred to as scientists, in so-called primitive societies. All we know is that attitudes can vary enormously. To refer again to the Pacific coast communities I mentioned a moment ago, they have, or rather had, since they no longer exist, artists specializing in different kinds of work and who were known by name and enjoyed a certain reputation, and from whom the nobles ordered pieces of sculpture or paintings, which they alone could afford to buy and that they paid for not in money, but in slaves or goods, and at prices such as Matisse or Picasso might command in our time. Compare this situation with the one that existed in a different region, which was nevertheless one of the greatest centres of artistic creativeness – I mean the Sepik basin in New Guinea. In that area, there are still some communities – but not all – in which everybody is a sculptor; the men spend their spare time sculpting; no doubt they are not all equally talented, but all are capable of producing the kind of objects we put in our museums. So you see that aesthetic creativeness can take widely different forms.

G.C. If we add that progress, which is something that seems to have a meaning for us, or to which we attribute a meaning, has no meaning in the societies you study.

C.L.-S. Agreed.

G.C. It would make no sense for them.

C.L.-S. Definitely not. Each of these societies considers that its essential and ultimate aim is to persevere in its existing form and carry on as it was established by its ancestors, and for the sole reason that it was so fashioned by its ancestors. There is no need for any further justification; 'that is how we have always done it' is the reply we receive without fail whenever we ask an informant the reason for a particular custom or institution. The fact that it exists is its only justification. It is legitimate because it has endured.

G.C. So, whereas progress, in Western societies, means evolution, change, and nothing more ...

C.L.-S. Yes, but because Western societies operate on the basis of differences in potential and internal differentials.

G.C. But in that case is progress in Western societies not entirely determined? Is it not completely beyond human control? Is it not entirely a function of the development of knowledge, and therefore entirely determined by knowledge? Is there not a built-in determinism within knowledge and methods of knowledge, which renders us powerless?

C.L.-S. That would seem to be the case, because, if someone were to ask us to state openly whether we were for or against certain kinds of progress – and the problem arises at the moment with the development of atomic energy – it is at least conceivable that a large number of people might say : 'No, it would be better not to have that; it would be better to stay as we are.' The fact of owning a car does not seem to me to be an advantage in itself; it is an indispensable form of defence in a society in which many other people have cars; but if I could choose, and if all my contemporaries would agree to give up their cars too, I would drive mine to the scrap-heap with great relief!

G.C. Just so. And now I fully realize that I am moving a long way away from anthropology, but this is a question that, as a non-specialist, an ordinary man, I feel I must ask myself: how could man intervene in what appears to be an inevitable process in no way dependent on us but only on knowledge itself? I am thinking, for instance, of all those attitudes which are usually considered as being related to a principle of generosity. They are always futile, always completely useless. What happens is always some kind of economic or technical progress, which makes it possible to achieve something that had previously been advocated by man's generous instincts, but which those instincts could never have brought into being on their own. In practice, it is the setting up of a market in some particular place which makes it possible for people to obtain the goods they were asking for, but as long as the conditions required for the setting up of a market did not exist, they could have gone on indefinitely claiming this material advantage in the name of the rights of man, there was never the faintest chance of their obtaining it. And this line of argument can be applied in all fields.

C.L.-S. Don't you think that this kind of helplessness shown by man when faced with human problems is, to a very large extent, the result of the enormous demographic expansion of modern societies? It is conceivable that small communities, small groups consisting of a few tens of thousands of people, or at most of a few hundreds of thousands, should be able to reflect on their situation and take conscious and considered decisions with a view to changing it. Our present inability to act is due, it seems to me, to the hugeness of the human mass within which we live, because even national groupings have been transcended and we are now tending more and more towards the creation of what is virtually a world civilization, and it is this new order of greatness, this change of scale in the dimensions of human society, which makes humanity unmanageable.

G.C. Yes, but at the same time it seems to me that the demographic expansion to which you refer also increases power to some extent, and that the problems continue to be dealt with by a minority, and that however important the difficulties you mention, they are not the only ones affecting the issue.

C.L.-S. I am unable to suggest an answer, and, what is more, I don't think anyone has an answer to suggest – least of all the anthropologist. In his effort to discover the difference between the societies he studies and other societies, over and above the presence or absence of writing, over and above the presence or absence of the category of history as a means of self-knowledge indispensable for a given society ... I don't of course, mean to assert absolutely that primitive societies have no past, but that their members feel no need to refer to the category of history; for them, it is devoid of meaning since, if a given thing has not always existed, it is in their eyes illegitimate, whereas, for us, the opposite is the case.

G.C. The opposite.

C.L.-S. This being so, we have to bring into play a phenomenon of a different kind. I mean the existence, on the level of the society itself, of inter-personal relations. The smallness of the population of these societies means that in fact, or at any rate in theory, it is possible for all the members of the social body to get to know each other, whereas beyond a certain figure of population, this is clearly impossible.

G.C. In our societies, 'to know' can be replaced by 'to accept the existence of'. A kind of *a priori* 'knowledge' could be maintained in our societies, whereby I accept the existence of all others just as readily as I do the existence of those I know best.

C.L.-S. We are well aware that there is a difference in kind and not simply in degree between the running of a town council and that of a parliament: in the case of the town council, decisions are not taken primarily in terms of a particular ideological content, but are also based on the knowledge of what Tom, Dick or Harry think and, above all, of what they are actually like. It is possible to get a total view of the varieties of human behaviour. Admittedly, ideas also come into play, but these can be interpreted in terms of the life history of each member of the small community – his family situation or his profession – whereas beyond a certain size of population, it is impossible to take this kind of detailed information into account. I have called this elsewhere the problem of levels of authority. Of course, even in Western societies, there are levels of authenticity in the form of institutional or non-institutional groups in which individual members have concrete knowledge of each other. But non-authentic levels are on the increase: I mean all those ways in which actual people are cut off from each other or interconnected only through intermediary agents or a system of relays, such as administrative machinery or ideological ramifications. In short, if the anthropologist were to make so bold as to play the reformer and say: 'This is how our experience of thousands of societies can be of use to you, the men of today!' he would no doubt advocate decentralization in all fields, so that the greatest number of social and economic activities could be carried out on the level of authenticity at which the members of a given group have a concrete knowledge of each other.

G.C. Could this concrete knowledge of individuals by each other not be made up for to a certain extent by the creation of a myth about man which would be valid for the whole of humanity and would make it possible to achieve *the most authentic form of authenticity possible?*

C.L.-S. But this is a contradiction in terms! In my view, the words 'myth' and 'authenticity' are quite incompatible with each other.

G.C. Yes, of course. That is why I said 'made up for to a certain extent'.

C.L.-S. This is out of the question. Myth is the most fundamental form of inauthenticity. I defined authenticity as the concrete nature of the knowledge people have of each other, and contrary to what might seem to be the case there is nothing more abstract than myths. Myths depend on propositions which, when we try to analyse them, force us to resort to symbolical logic. It is not absolutely without reason – although I am referring to a non-technical use of the word – that 'myth' and 'mystification' have a great deal in common.

G.C. Yes, they are similar. But, in the last resort, whatever degree of decentralization may be achieved, if we take into account the steady increase in size of the existing masses of population, there is no reason to suppose that the concrete relationships you are referring to will be established. It will therefore be necessary to replace them by something else.

C.L.-S. Yes, but that is not the function of the anthropologist. I am making a great concession (I would not care to put it into writing, but in the course of a conversation one is tempted to say things that one would not put into writing) in trying to offer the reformer a helping hand, but I could never do any more than touch the tip of his fingers. I don't know what the possibilities are. Inevitably, circumstances have made anthropologists the unworthy repositories of a vast amount of sociological and philosophical experience – the experience of the so-called primitive societies to whom writing was unknown, which is gradually being wiped out and which it is our function to preserve as far as possible. And if you say to me: 'What lesson have you drawn from it?', this is the answer I would give, for what it is worth.

But whether or not this lesson can be of use to modern man, or to the men of the future, I have no idea.

V

ART AND THE GROUP

GEORGES CHARBONNIER. What difference does the anthropologist tend to see between the art of so-called primitive societies and, if not 'modern' art, the art of 'modern times'?

CLAUDE LÉVI-STRAUSS. First of all, it is advisable to make a distinction within the rather vague category of modern times. An anthropologist would feel perfectly at ease, and on familiar ground, with Greek art before the fifth century B.C. and even with Italian painting, at least up to the time of the school of Siena. Where we might feel on less safe ground and might get an impression of strangeness would be with fifth-century Greek art and Italian painting from the Quattrocento onwards. It is with these relatively 'modern' forms, each one being taken in its historical dimension, that we must attempt a comparison with primitive art, or rather arts.

This having been established, it seems to me that the difference is related to facts of two quite different kinds: on the one hand, what might be called the individualization of artistic output and, on the other, its increasingly figurative or representational character. And here again, I would like to be more explicit:

when I refer to the individualization of artistic production, I am not thinking first and foremost of the personality of the artist as an individual or as a creator. In many so-called primitive societies, the artist also has these characteristics, although it was a long time before we became aware of the fact. Recent studies in connection with African sculpture have shown that the sculptor is an artist who is well known and whose fame may sometimes have spread very far afield, so that the native public was able to recognize the individual style of each maker of masks or statues. In the case of modern art it is the art-loving public, rather than the artist, that has shown an increasing trend towards individualization. It is no longer the group as a whole which looks to the artist to provide it with certain objects, fashioned in accordance with prescribed rules, but art-lovers – however bizarre the term may appear when we are making a comparison with societies very different from ours – or groups of art-lovers.

G.C. In our day, there are several reasons why art should be the special preserve of art-lovers. First of all, there is a definite split within the group, since one section of it shows no interest at all in works of art, or to all intents and purposes accepts only the lowest forms of art. But there is also an economic problem : in Western societies the work of art is a very expensive commodity, and consequently is not available to everyone. Does this phenomenon sometimes occur in primitive societies, or is it quite unknown there? In primitive societies, is the work of art within everyone's reach?

C.L.-S. It depends. There are some primitive societies in which the social and economic phenomena you have just referred to do occur, and where artists work for rich people or rich groups, who pay them handsomely, and even derive great prestige from the fact that they have managed to secure the services of a particular artist. This does happen, but admittedly it is exceptional. However, you are right to raise the question of social hierarchy, because I think we are going to come across it again in this connection, just as we met it the other day when we were discussing the idea of progress and the place of history. We said that history is a category inherent in certain societies, a way in which stratified societies apprehend their own being, and not a social environment within which all human groups are placed on the same footing. We are now going to come across very similar ideas again.

But I would not like to adopt this explanation uncritically, because I think that if we accept it immediately we shall find it less convincing than if we arrive at it by some roundabout route. I continue, then, with what I was saying about the two features – the individualization of artistic output, considered from the art-lover's, rather than the artist's, viewpoint, and the increasingly figurative or representational nature of the works. It seems to me that, in the so-called primitive arts, owing to the rather rudimentary technological skills of the people concerned, there is always a disparity between the technical means at the artist's disposal and the resistance of the materials he has to master, and this prevents him, as it were, even if his conscious intention were different – and more often than not it isn't – from turning the work of art into a straightforward copy. He cannot, or does not wish to, *reproduce* his model in its entirety, and he is therefore obliged to suggest its *sign-value*. His art, instead of being representational, is a system of signs. Yet on reflection, it seems quite clear that the two phenomena – the individualization of art on the one hand and the disappearance or diminution of the function of the work as a sign system on the other – are functionally linked, and the reason for this is simple: for language to exist, there must be a group. It goes without saying that language ...

G.C. Being a constituent element ...

C.L.-S. ... is a group phenomenon; it is a constituent element of the group; it can only exist through the group, since language cannot be modified or disrupted at will. We would never manage to understand each other if, within our society, we formed a series of coteries, each one of which had its own particular language, or if we allowed constant changes and revolutions to take place in language, like those that we have been able to observe now for a number of years in the fine arts. Language is, then, a general phenomenon which concerns the whole community, and it is, above all, a phenomenon with a very relative, but nevertheless very great, stability.

The two differences we noted a moment ago are, therefore, two aspects of one and the same reality. In so far as an element of individualization is introduced into art, inevitably and automatically the semantic function of the work tends to disappear, to be replaced by an increasingly closer approximation to the model, which the artist tries to imitate instead of merely signifying it.

Having made this point, I am quite ready to return now to the sociological observations you made a moment ago. We established a relationship between art and language, or at least with the various sign-systems. This is a question we had already raised in connection with writing. When we inquired with what major social phenomenon the appearance of writing was linked, we agreed, I think, that, at all times and in all places, the only social reality accompanying writing was the appearance of divisions and cleavages corresponding to caste, or class systems, since writing, in its early phase, seems to have been a means whereby men were reduced to a state of bondage by other men, a means of governing men and gaining possession of material things.

Now, it is perhaps no accident that the transformation of art to which I alluded a moment ago occurred in societies acquainted with writing – I am not saying that writing was a new phenomenon at the time of the Renaissance, but the invention of printing was new, i.e. writing was now on quite a different scale in relation to the social life of the community – and, at any rate, in two societies, the Athenian city state and the Florentine city state, class distinctions, and differences of wealth, were very much in evidence; in short, these were societies in which art became, up to a point, something that was enjoyed by a minority who were using it as an instrument, or means, of private pleasure, much more than it has ever been, or still is, in the so-called primitive societies, where it is a system of communication operating throughout the entire group.

G.C. What is very clear is that, in Western societies, all artists are unanimous in deploring the fact that their works are not widely circulated at the so-called popular level. Yet, at the same time, this feeling never amounts to much more than a vague expression of regret.

C.L.-S. But it is bound to be vague because an historical situation, which has taken centuries to develop, obviously cannot suddenly change just because artists in general – or any particular artist – want it to change. All we can do is take note of a situation which exists and which it is not in our power to change.

G.C. But where have we to look for the causes of the break? Within the group itself, or in a change in the function of art which is linked with other phenomena?

C.L.-S. I think the causes are to be found in a general development of civilization, which did not take place all at once, since at some periods there are reversals to early stages. Art, so it seems to me, abandoned its function as a sign-system in Greek statuary, and then again in Italian painting of the Renaissance. But it might be claimed, up to a point, that the phenomenon is observable in embryonic form in other societies, and probably occurred in connection with Egyptian statuary, although to a lesser degree than in Greece; perhaps during a certain period in Assyrian statuary, too, and lastly in pre-Columbian Mexico, a society that anthropologists are particularly concerned with although it has some points in common with the other societies I have just mentioned. Now, it is probably not an accident that I should think of pre-Columbian Mexico in discussing the variations that have occurred in the production of art, since the Mexicans were also a people who had a form of writing. I believe that writing played a very significant part in the evolution of art in the direction of the figurative, since writing taught men that signs could be used not only to signify the external world but also to apprehend it, to gain possession of it. I will not be so naive as to claim that a Greek statue of the classical period was an exact representation of the human body. There is a sense in which it too is remote from the model; as in the case of an African statue, although to a lesser degree, we are dealing with signs. It follows that the difference occurs not only on this level, but also in the attitudes of the artist and the public. It seems to me that in

Greek statuary, or in Italian painting of the Renaissance, at least from the Quattrocento onwards, the artist's attitude to his model is characterized not only by an attempt to signify, i.e. by the purely intellectual approach which is so striking a feature of so-called primitive art, but also – although I may seem to be uttering a paradox – by an almost covetous attitude which seems to be related to magic, since art is based on the illusion of being able not only to communicate with the being, but also to possess it through the medium of the effigy. I would term this: 'possessiveness with regard to the object', a way of taking possession of some phenomenon of great external value or beauty. It is this avid and ambitious desire to take possession of the object for the benefit of the owner or even of the spectator which seems to me to constitute one of the outstandingly original features of the art of Western civilization.

VI

THREE DIFFERENCES

GEORGES CHARBONNIER. Claude Lévi-Strauss, during the last broadcast, you talked about the individualization of art: you used the words 'collective' and 'individual' several times, and this naturally leads me to wonder what connection there is between the two terms. Are they opposites, or are they complementary to each other? What do they imply within their sociological context? And lastly I am led to ask myself a rather different question: is the distinction between the individual and the collective – it should be remembered that we are concerned with the conditions in which works of art are produced – equally valid – supposing it is valid in itself – within primitive societies and Western societies?

CLAUDE LÉVI-STRAUSS. The distinction between the individual and the collective, which appears so clear to us, has very little significance as regards the conditions in which works of art are created in primitive societies. There are, in primitive societies, well-known artists who have a recognized style. They are sought out in preference to other artists, and there is no doubt that they receive higher payment.

Furthermore, the artist often tries to satisfy

E   65 individual needs. Take, for instance, the primitive Indian societies to be found in the States of Bastar and Orissa, and which consist of Mongolian communities of more or less mixed ancestry. Some of these societies have a very highly developed kind of painting in the form of mural painting, the function of which is essentially magical and religious; it is intended for the curing of certain diseases and forecasting the future; or, to put it more accurately, when an individual finds himself in a critical situation, either physical or mental, and wants to get out of it, he calls in a sorcerer, who is also a painter, and who comes and decorates the wall of his house with large patterns, which are not always overtly representational. The sorcerer is, therefore, a person with a recognized talent, not only as a healer and soothsayer, but also as a painter. He goes to his client's house the day before he is to carry out his task. He is very handsomely paid; he is his client's guest, and during the night he spends in the house, he has a dream, the various episodes and details of which he records with minute care on one of the walls of the house.

On the other hand, the work he creates does not emerge from the depths of his own individual unconscious, but obeys extremely strict rules; the foreign observer, who looks at these pictures from the outside, might consider them all to be the work of the same man: there are no great differences between them which might indicate how old they are, within a range of fifty years. So here we have an almost inextricable intermingling of the most highly individual conditions of artistic creation, on the one hand, with the most sociological and collective, on the other. The two aspects are indissolubly linked as if, by deliberately and systematically leaving the task of creating the work to the unconscious activity of the mind – it is a dream, after all – a point were reached at which the distinction between the individual and the collective tended to disappear. We are therefore led to wonder whether the value and significance of the distinction ought not to be limited to one particular kind of art which is located at a certain level of deliberate and conscious activity – a more superficial level, as it were, of mental activity – whereas the so-called primitive societies are capable of a more objective acceptance of the part played by the unconscious in aesthetic creation, and handle the obscure functions of the mind with extraordinary lucidity.

G.C. So, in your view, the distinction is confined to Western societies?

C.L.-S. I would say that the distinction is relevant within Western societies, and ceases to be so in widely different societies.

This, then, is the first difference – the relevance or irrelevance of the distinction between individual and collective creation. A second difference (of course, you will tell me that it is no longer valid at the present time, but I will come back to that later – for the moment, let us concentrate on the point of divergence) is the contrast between a kind of art which aims above all at signification, and another kind of art which, in aiming at what a little while ago I called 'possessiveness', has for a long time been increasingly representational in character and less and less of a sign-system.

Finally, there is a third difference: I see it as the very conscious and systematic tendency on the part of aesthetic activity to become progressively more shut in upon itself, that is, to stand, not in a direct relationship with objects, but in relation to artistic tradition: 'the example of the great masters', 'to paint in the style of the masters'. Here again, we have a distinction which is not relevant to primitive art, because the problem could never arise, since the continuity of the tradition is assured. We can thus define three concentric zones with three corresponding kinds of centripetal movements tending to turn art in upon itself and make it into a world of its own: individualism, representationalism, and what might be called academicism. Now, you were asking me the question: does modern art ...

G.C. None of the terms will apply?

C.L.-S. They will no longer apply, but in what sense? The first modern revolution was – you are forcing me to talk of matters I know nothing about and in which you are a specialist – well, can we perhaps say it was Impressionism?

G.C. Yes, that would seem to be the first truly external

and overt manifestation, as far as the spectator was concerned.

C.L.-S. Truly, I have no intention of venturing into a field which is not my own. I am judging the situation as a whole from the outside and from the sociological point of view, that is, by treating revolutions in painting as if they were transformations which not only affected the structure of works of art but also led to certain repercussions within the group, and it seems to me that Impressionism corresponds more closely to this tendency towards ...

G.C. I don't consider myself as a specialist in these matters, and I feel obviously less well equipped than the anthropologist, yet I feel absolutely in agreement with you when you say that Impressionism is the external and visible manifestation ...

C.L.-S. Take the Impressionist painter: what is he trying to do? It seems to me that his particular revolution is strictly limited to the third of the differences I described a moment ago. What he is really trying to do is to escape from the academic vision of the object; he is anxious that the object he is depicting, the model he is using, should not be the model as represented by previous masters, but the real object, 'in the raw'. Is it possible to say this?

G.C. Yes, perfectly possible.

C.L.-S. Only, this raw object is still an object to be represented, reproduced and appropriated.

G.C. However, there is still some claim to see the object as the physicist sees it.

C.L.-S. Yes, of course.

G.C. People read Fresnel and try to use his theories; they almost believe that, when painting, they are studying physics.

C.L.-S. So, in a sense, it is a reactionary revolution : it is a revolution, since the previous conventions have been overthrown, yet the crux of the problem has been missed – the crux, or deeper problem, related to the semantic nature of the work of art. The 'possessive-representative' aspect survives intact in Impressionism, and the Impressionist revolution is superficial and only skin-deep, whatever incidental importance it may have for us. I say this without trying to diminish the greatness of the Impressionist painters, whom I admire as much as you do.

G.C. In any case, Impressionist painting does not penetrate below the surface, for the simple reason, perhaps, that it is more interested in the surface than in anything else; the surface of the object is what it is interested in; the decomposition of light at the instant when it comes into contact with the object.

c.l.-s. Yes, but there is more to it than that. If I wanted to pursue the argument along these lines, I would say that you cannot consider Impressionism purely from the point of view of form and that the subject-matter of Impressionist painting is also of considerable importance.

g.c. The Impressionists did not attack the object in a fundamental way.

c.l.-s. Allow me to adopt a more superficial approach than yours. What strikes me about the Impressionists is not only the change in style, but also the change in subject-matter : their sudden predilection for humble, suburban landscapes or the often unattractive countryside near towns – a field, say, or a single line of trees – and it seems to me that these features represent quite a considerable change, in comparison with what not only Poussin but even the Romantics understood by a 'landscape', which had to be a sublime setting with mountains, waterfalls, ancient trees and so on.

g.c. Yes, but there is a general trend which can be observed in all the arts, a hundred years after Impressionism, that is, right up till the present day, and which, generally speaking, consists in making the hero keep his feet on this earth – in taking the hero and putting him into the Underground, since that is where he lives.

c.l.-s. Of course, and it is because the unspoilt world

of Nature that artists could give themselves the luxury of painting in the seventeenth and eighteenth centuries, and even at the beginning of the nineteenth, is tending to disappear because of the advance of mechanization – bridges, railways and urban development – and so mankind must be taught to be satisfied with the small change of nature, which is all that is left to them of the great Nature which has now been lost for ever. In Impressionism, there is this didactic purpose, an attempt to act as the guide of civilization.

G.C. The Impressionists magnified what was being minimized.

C.L.-S. Yes, or rather they tried to exploit more intensively, as it were, the diminished area that was still at their disposal. Broadly speaking, I think we both agree that, as regards form, the Impressionist revolution was confined to the last-mentioned contrast: a return to the pure and naked object, which was no longer the object as seen through the eyes of the masters, yet without realizing that this was not the essential problem; the essential problem is to know whether the object is being signified or reproduced, or at least which of the two aims the artist has in view since, in actual fact, the object can never be reproduced.

Cubism, on the other hand, continues the same revolution but grapples with the second difference. It rediscovered the semantic truth of art, for its essential ambition was to signify and not just to represent.

So the Cubist revolution was more profound than the Impressionist revolution, although in the first instance it made use of the results achieved by Impressionism. Cubism went beyond the object to signification. Only there is always something basic lacking in Cubism, which prevents us establishing an equivalence between it and the primitive arts – even though there was nothing accidental in the fact that the Cubists drew their inspiration from the primitive arts, and had a liking for them, and even though we feel that primitive works of art can coexist more easily and happily with Cubism than with other forms of painting.

G.C. Yes, and they cannot conceivably coexist with Impressionist art. You simply cannot put a Sisley alongside a piece of African sculpture. The juxtaposition is unthinkable.

C.L.-S. Because the Cubists drew inspiration from primitive art and, in a sense, understood what such art could teach them and the help they could get from it. Nevertheless, there is one basic difficulty which Cubism cannot overcome: you referred to it a moment ago. The conditions of artistic output remain individualistic, and Cubism, on its own, cannot recreate the collective function of the work of art. If we accept my hypothesis of the three differences, we can see that – by a kind of regressive movement – Impressionism succeeded in overcoming the third and most superficial difference; Cubism overcame the second and intermediary difference; but there is still one difference left, and it is the most profound, the one which, over and above the question of aesthetic forms, concerns the place assigned to art in society. It seems to me that sufficient thought has not been given to this point, and that it might offer a means of explaining a comparatively recent and surprising phenomenon – I mean the extraordinary abundance of 'styles' adopted by one and the same painter, and which is exemplified, for example, in the whole of Picasso's work, the radical change in style every ...

G.C. It is becoming increasingly evident that changes in style, in our day, can be associated with three great names ...

C.L.-S. Yes.

G.C. Roughly speaking, the painters concerned are Picasso, Masson and Picabia; they certainly go in for constant changes in style

C.L.-S. But it is not only painters who change their style. In the musical world, there is a certain analogy between Stravinsky and Picasso.

G.C. Yes.

C.L.-S. In Stravinsky, too, we find constant changes in style, and so the phenomenon is in a sense a sociological one, in my view directly linked with – and the immediate consequence of – the individualization of

artistic output; it is as if Cubism, being unable to overcome the opposition, or the contrast, between the
artist and the spectator (and more especially between
the artist and the buyer, for the buyer is obviously the
'operative' spectator) succeeded only in exchanging
one kind of academicism for another. The academicism of pre-Impressionist painting was, to use the
language of the linguists, *an academicism of the
signified*: the objects the artist was trying to reproduce – the human face, flowers, or a vase – were seen
in terms of a particular convention and tradition;
whereas with the abundance of styles which occurred
at a certain period and at a certain point in the work
of contemporary creative artists, academicism of the
signified disappears, to be replaced by a new kind of
academicism which I will call *the academicism of the
signifier*. This is, in fact, the academicism of language
itself, since in the case of both Stravinsky and Picasso,
we observe an almost obsessional consumption of all
the sign-systems which have been, or still are, in use
in the human race, anywhere and everywhere, ever
since men have had a form of artistic expression.
Academicism of language replaces academicism of
subject-matter, because, since the conditions of artistic production remain individualistic, there is no possibility whatever of a true language being established,
since language (I come back to my starting-point) is a
group phenomenon and therefore a stable phenomenon.

G.C. Yes, but in a way we might say that this was

due to ease – perhaps not so much of translation as of transmission and dissemination: communications have improved, but that does not mean simply that man has been able to travel, it also means that he has had the opportunity to extend his knowledge, to read and to look at works of art in reproduction: for there is one phenomenon which is as important as writing in this connection: this is photography.

C.L.-S. Of course!

G.C. The Cubist painter was able – and from the period when individualization began to develop, any artist has been able – to acquaint himself with all that had been achieved before his time; he can now learn other languages.

C.L.-S. No – not learn them ... I wouldn't say that he learns them; it is not so much a question of learning as of imitating them ...

G.C. Of seeing how they work.

C.L.-S. ... of giving a completely illusory transfiguration of them, since all there is to go on is the external semblance of the sign: the message is obviously no longer present, and I am using the word message, not in the metaphysical sense, but with the meaning it has in communication theory.

G.C. Every painter has become an expert.

C.L.-S. Yes, but I don't think that is enough; if you consider the artists in so-called primitive societies, they too know what is going on in the world outside. Of course, they don't know what happened twenty thousand years before their time, nor do they know what is happening twenty thousand miles away, but they are acquainted with the art of their nearest neighbours, which may be as different from their own as Egyptian art from Gothic or Baroque. But their attitude is not one of assimilation; on the contrary it is one of rejection, since they are anxious to protect their own 'language', for the good reason that if the art of primitive societies assimilated external elements too liberally and too readily, the semantic function of the art, its role inside the society, would break down. So you see, the abundance of styles found in certain contemporary artists or creators does not involve the assimilation of foreign idioms so much as a sort of gratuitous playing about with artistic languages.

G.C. But I still think it necessary to emphasize the fact – I apologize for coming back to this point – that this is after all a phenomenon characteristic of very few men, and only of the greatest exponents of each kind of art: changes in style are most obvious in great artists like Picasso, or Giacometti.

C.L.-S. I agree with you, but I cannot see any fundamental difference between what might be called the two *impasses* in which contemporary painting is now caught: first, the blind alley in which Picasso finds himself and where he is forced to juggle with a succession of different styles, because the signs have nothing more than the formal function of a sign-system : actually, and sociologically speaking, they do not operate as a means of communication within a given group; secondly, the experiments of the abstract artists who do not, each on his own account, multiply the number of sign-systems, each one of whom tries to analyse his own system, to break it down and exhaust it completely, thus emptying it of any signifying function by removing from it even the possibility of signifying. It seems to me that both procedures are desperate and complementary forms of artistic activity.

G.C. But there is one astonishing point: going back over what you have just said, I recall that you established three fundamental differences, did you not?

C.L.-S. Yes.

G.C. Then you considered the phenomenon of modern art – not the art of modern times, but contemporary art. You expressed the opinion that Impressionism succeeded in overcoming the first difficulty which faced modern art, and that Cubism was able to overcome the second. Now, in a sense, Cubism was already contained in Impressionism, was it not?

C.L.-S. Yes.

G.C. And abstract art was, in a way, contained in Cubism. Might there not be an *a priori* case – before any critical appraisal – for thinking that abstract art was on the point of overcoming the third difficulty? Yet it is precisely abstract art which, in your view, is in the most hopeless *impasse*.

C.L.-S. No, I don't believe that abstract art is capable of achieving this, although obviously it would be very tempting to work out a symmetrical pattern ...

G.C. It would be too good to be true!

C.L.-S. Yes.

G.C. Only, in that case I wonder how ...

C.L.-S. All the same, you know, the three differences ...

G.C. Just when my hopes were highest! ...

C.L.-S. Yes?

G.C. I am told – no ...

C.L.-S. But at this point I would like to counter your statement by asserting that a distinction or even a scale of values should be introduced into the three contrasts I listed a short while ago. The last two diffi-culties, which have been overcome, belong to what the Marxists would call the superstructure, whereas the first, that is the collective function of the work of art, belongs to the infrastructure. A purely formal development, or the dynamic force inherent in aesthetic creation, is not enough to overcome it. At the point where we come up against this contrast, art is, if you will allow me to use the expression, geared to sociological reality, and shows itself to be powerless to change it. It is in this sense that I am conscious of an *impasse*.

G.C. Which you do not observe only in painting?

C.L.-S. No, I do not observe it only in painting; it seems to me to be just as unmistakable in music.

G.C. Do you also see it in literature, in the written word?

C.L.-S. In poetry, yes, and very likely in the novel too ... I don't know why I am limiting it ... Yes, it seems to me – and this strikes me as being quite a commonplace observation, which has been made by people other than myself – that we have reached a sort of *impasse*, and realize that we are tired of listening to the kind of music we have always listened to, looking at the kind of painting we are used to looking at every day and of reading books written according to the patterns we are familiar with. All this has given rise to a kind of unhealthy tension, unhealthy precisely because it is too self-conscious, and arises from experimentation and a determination to discover something new, whereas major unheavals of this kind, if they are to be fruitful, occur at a much less conscious level than that at which they are happening at the present time, when people are trying deliberately and systematically to invent new forms, and that in my view is precisely the sign of a state of crisis ...

G.C. But it is a crisis so deep-rooted that it might end, if I understand you rightly, in the complete disappearance of all that we call art forms? ... In the first place, by indicating their uselessness?

C.L.-S. You know that from the anthropological point of view – which I am certainly wrong to allow myself to be persuaded by you to abandon – from an anthropological point of view, this would not be in the least monstrous or shocking. After all, art has not always played such an important part in human societies; we know of some societies which are artistically very rich, and others which are extremely poor in this respect.

G.C. Undoubtedly. Besides, there are pointers which suggest that all you have said is true. We need look no further, for instance, than the determination, expressed by all creative artists in all fields, to achieve absolute integration of their life and work, so that the two can no longer be separated. This is a definite sign of a kind of desperation. Artaud wants his poetry to be himself, the painter wants the picture to be himself, the musician wants the sound to be himself, so that there can be no severing of a body and an image, a body and a colour, a body and a sound, a body and a word.

C.L.-S. Yes, but, it seems to me ...

G.C. Is it because they all think that colours, sounds and images are eluding their grasp?

C.L.-S. It could be an indication that, since subject-matter is beginning to be wanting, artists are resorting to all kinds of expedients.

G.C. However, this leads us to ask a question ... I am ready to accept the fact that all forms are doomed to disappear, that art itself has become ...

C.L.-S. Of course, the disappearance would be temporary. We are judging the situation according to the time-scale of our own lives!

G.C. Yes, yes, agreed, but in that case I move on at once to another question: what is the function of art? Is it possible to deduce the function of art in contemporary societies from what it is in primitive societies? And could I thus arrive at the conclusion that all forms of art have become useless in our society, and that something is yet to emerge which will perhaps not be a form of art? Or, on the contrary, is the extinction of art something quite natural, so that no one will even notice its disappearance?

c.l.-s. I cannot take it upon myself to forecast the future, but I would like to call your attention to an omission in what I was saying a moment ago and which, in a sense, makes it possible to put the question in a wider form. I said that, in every aesthetic creation, there was some kind of disparity between the technical means at the artist's disposal and the resistance of the actual process of creation – let us say the resistance of the material – and that although the extent of the disparity varied from one society to another, it was always present and imposed on art an essentially signifying function. When the artist cannot produce a facsimile of the model, he is content, or he deliberately chooses, to signify it. I would like to add that the disparity I am referring to is not solely caused by the means the artist has at his disposal. These may be inadequate, which is generally the case in so-called primitive arts, taking primitive in the widest possible sense – that is, including the Italian primitives as well as the art of primitive peoples. On the other hand, there may be what I will call a super-abundance of the object, and this seems to me to be a very striking feature of the arts and crafts of primitive peoples, since we cannot say that it is invariably because of inadequate technical means that the signifying function occurs. There are so-called primitive communities which attain extraordinary technical mastery in the practice of their creative skills; you know that pre-Columbian Peruvian pottery is among the most perfect achievements of the potter's art, and that ancient Peruvian weaving is unsurpassed. But among the so-called primitive peoples, there is always a superabundance of the object which re-creates the margin of disparity, and which is to be explained by the fact that the world in which these people live is, for the most part, a supernatural world. Being supernatural, it is by definition non-representable, since no 'facsimile' or model of it can be provided. So, either through deficiency or excess, the model is always wide of the representation, and the exigencies of art always exceed the means at the artist's disposal. In this respect, it seems to me that there is something – how shall I say? – disquieting, perhaps, for the future of art in the development of contemporary societies: thanks to scientific knowledge, we have succeeded in 'reducing' objects to a very considerable extent. All that we can learn about the nature of objects, through scientific investigation, represents a corresponding diminution and loss of aesthetic appreciation, whereas primitive peoples ...

G.C. That is very true.

C.L.-S. ... who have little or no scientific knowledge ...

G.C. The artist's sphere of activity is being reduced, and this incidentally is one of the subjects I would like to discuss ...

C.L.-S. Yes, indeed, the object is much more important,

objects are heavier, denser, imbued with a number of things that we have eliminated from them.

G.C. You have whittled away the artist's material.

C.L.-S. Whom do you mean by 'you'?

G.C. Scientists! There is no doubt about it, I am sure! But a moment ago, you said – if I have understood your terminology correctly – that the signifying function arose from the existence of a disparity. I am wondering if the signifying function is not now being maintained thanks to an impossibility, and one which resides chiefly in the fact that you are reducing the margins within which the artist can operate; you are limiting his field of activity and he is inevitably discovering how more and more impossible it is for him to exist, and the new kind of despair experienced by the artist – which is much more real, I think, than the despair that was talked about twenty years ago – springs from the fact that he does not feel he has any legitimate place in society, or anything to say or to see; but he is nevertheless succeeding in wresting forms from all these impossibilities. To take an example from the theatre – one of the greatest living dramatists, Samuel Beckett, is surely someone who expresses precisely what we are now saying?

C.L.-S. I cannot join you in a theatrical discussion, because – and I apologize for the fact – I am allergic to the theatre. When I go to the theatre, I always have the impression of having inadvertently strayed into the flat on the floor below and of overhearing a conversation which doesn't concern me, and moreover doesn't interest me. So let us leave the theatre out of it. Although ...

G.C. This is to reduce the artist's field of activity still further!

C.L.-S. Although in a sense the problem is the same, and it is the extremely figurative 'fac-simile' aspect of the theatre – the fact that the men and women walking about on the stage are real, when what I ask of art is that it should offer me an escape from human society and entry into a different kind of society – here, too, he would eventually find ourselves dealing with the problem of signification.

G.C. But, if we set aside the theatre, has the subject-matter of the artist not become, precisely, the very impossibility of his existence?

C.L.-S. Yes, I believe you are quite right.

G.C. It is true as far as poetry is concerned: Artaud fits the definition.

C.L.-S. Yes, contemporary art tends towards non-being – the subject-matter disappears altogether and tends to be no more than a system of signs.

G.C. Subject-matter has lost its massivity.

C.L.-S. I agree with you. Only, this increases and ex-acerbates the contradiction inherent in contemporary art, because (and this seems to me to be a typical feature of abstract painters) we are left with nothing but a system of signs, but 'outside language', since the sign-system is created by a single individual, and he is liable to change his system fairly frequently.

VII

NATURAL ART AND CULTURAL ART

GEORGES CHARBONNIER. Claude Lévi-Strauss, before we leave the comparison between the art of primitive societies and that of contemporary Western societies, I would like to remind you of an observation you made to me on one occasion: we were talking about the function of art in general and about the fact that the elaboration of an additional reality is the characteristic effect of a work of art, and that it is through this effect that we can recognize a work of art. I had made a possibly rash remark: I had asked if it was the function of the artist to secrete reality. You pointed out to me that the expression 'to secrete reality' was at once too simple and ambiguous, and that any daub or scribble and, more generally speaking, any activity adds fresh reality to reality, without necessarily being a thing of beauty. Then you added: 'However, I must admit that the attitude of the Surrealists in this respect was disturbing.' What did you mean by this?

CLAUDE LÉVI-STRAUSS. I remember once having a long correspondence with André Breton on the subject. Is an absolutely original document automatically a work of art, because of its originality, or must there be something more to it? In so far as the work of art is a sign of the object and not a literal reproduction, it reveals something that was not immediately present in our perception of the object, and that is its structure, because the peculiar feature of the language of art is that there exists a profound homology between the structure of the signified and the structure of the signifier. In this respect, articulate language can signify in any way it chooses; there is no homology between the words and the objects to which they relate, or if we were to suppose there is, we would have to revert to those old ideas belonging to the philosophy of language, according to which liquid semi-vowels are particularly suited to the description of physical bodies in the liquid state, and we use very open vowels for heavy objects, and so on.

G.C. So you believe that the Surrealists were absolutely right to objectivize the object and turn it into a work of art? The chair which becomes an object by relinquishing its function as a chair is, then, a perfect realization of the coincidence between object and work of art.

C.L.-S. At any rate, this seems possible in so far as the work of art, in signifying the object, succeeds in creating a structure of signification which is in relation to the structure of the object.

G.C. So, coincidence, by definition, is implied in objectivization?

C.L.-S. The structure of the object to which I am referring is not present in immediate perception, and consequently the work of art makes it possible to achieve an advance in knowledge.

G.C. Is this progress achieved through objectivization or is it not? Things would be too easy, if the effect were achieved in advance!

C.L.-S. It is not necessarily achieved by objectivization, but it can be ... ; for instance, the very great painters like Ingres – it seems to me that Ingres's secret is that he could give the illusion of a fac-simile (we need only think of his Cashmere shawls reproduced with all the most minute details of design and shades of colour) while at the same time the apparent fac-simile reveals a signification which goes far beyond perception and even extends to the structure of the object of perception.

G.C. I think the Surrealists really played a very important part in this connection and, as regards the plastic arts, I think they had an equally important idea when they thought of what they called 'ready-mades': take, for instance, this microphone in front of me. I can decide that it is a piece of sculpture; it is ready made and it was deliberately created for a purpose, but I can decide that it is a work of art.

C.L.-S. And yet the feature of the 'ready-made' – you will correct me if I am wrong – seems to me to have been that it was very rarely reducible to a single object: in order to make a 'ready-made', there must be at least two objects.

G.C. A single object can be enough ... the famous bottle-drainer which Marcel Duchamp used, for instance.

C.L.-S. Even in this instance, it is not true, because it is not the same draining rack as it was in the cellar or the store-cupboard ...

G.C. Yes, of course, but that is what I mean!

C.L.-S. All right! You stand it on a piece of furniture, in a drawing-room ...

G.C. My aim is, precisely, to isolate it.

C.L.-S. ... and consequently it only becomes a work of art in the new context in which it is placed.

G.C. Quite, and because I have decided that it should be so.

C.L.-S. That's right.

G.C. In other words, it seems to me that, in this case, the opposite is happening: I am separating the signi-fied from the signifier.

C.L.-S. No.

G.C. I am not juxtaposing two structures.

C.L.-S. Yes you are!

G.C. It seems to me that I am separating one structure from another.

C.L.-S. I don't agree with you at all! The bottle-drainer in the cellar is a signifier of a certain signified: in other words, it is a device used for draining bottles. If you put it on a drawing-room mantelpiece, you obviously break and explode the relationship between signified and signifier ...

G.C. Bottles don't come into it any more!

C.L.-S. In doing this, you are bringing about a semantic fission.

G.C. Yes, that is what I mean.

C.L.-S. But the semantic fission helps to produce a fusion since, when you set the object alongside other objects, you bring out certain structural properties that it already possessed – properties of harmony or balance, or perhaps weirdness or aggressiveness – if it looks like the bony skeleton of a fish – you bring to light properties which were latent in it.

G.C. I quite agree, but by separating the signifier and the signified.

c.l.-s. But the separation serves to create an unexpected fusion between another signifier and another signified.

g.c. That I am quite prepared to accept, but nevertheless I began by separating them.

c.l.-s. You are thereby effecting, if you will allow me to use a pretentious expression, a different equalization of the relationship between signifier and signified, an equalization which existed in the realm of the possible but was not overtly expressed in the original situation of the object. You are therefore, in a sense, adding to human knowledge, you are discovering in the object latent properties which were not perceptible in the initial context; this is what the poet does every time he uses a word or an expression in an unusual way.

g.c. Of course. But, this being so, I am led to wonder whether, when he had this idea, Marcel Duchamp did not open up a limitless prospect. Who is to prevent me objectivizing any object whatever? Who is to prevent me considering any object as a 'ready-made'? Is this not a new way of arriving at reality by magnifying each thing so that it acquires the function of an art object?

c.l.-s. It should be stated, however, that not any object used any how will do; objects are not necessarily all equally rich in these latent possibilities; we are referring to certain objects in certain contexts.

G.C. Might it not be possible to generalize still further and say: any object in the widest possible context?

C.L.-S. Of course, I am perfectly convinced that it is possible to generalize and if I wanted – not, however, as an anthropologist – to predict what the painting of the future might be like in terms of my personal preferences, I would forecast that it will become anecdotal and extremely figurative (but cannot these terms, in one sense, be applied to as perfect a work as Poussin's 'Funérailles de Phocion'?) – that is, a kind of painting which, instead of trying to escape completely from the objective world which is, after all, the only world which interests us as human beings, or to be satisfied with the objective world in which modern man has his being and which does not strike me as very satisfactory either for the senses or for the mind, would, by using all the technical applications of the most traditional kind of painting, endeavour to re-create around me a more viable universe than the one in which I am living, not …

G.C. Ah! you are preserving the work of art, whereas I was supposing that if it were to disappear, it would be replaced by reality itself.

C.L.-S. Yes?

G.C. In the last analysis, if the artist disappears, the lesson to be learnt is perhaps that reality itself is a work of art; that no object has a special function nor is to be considered in a particular context.

C.L.-S. I am stressing the point because I think we are on the verge of what would be an extremely dangerous confusion: it is not every object in itself which is a work of art, but certain arrangements, or patterns, or relationships between objects. It is exactly the same thing as with the words of a language – in themselves they have very uncertain meanings, they are almost devoid of significance and only acquire a sense from their context; words such as 'flower' or 'stone' refer to an endless series of very vague objects and only take on their full meaning inside a given sentence. In the case of 'ready-mades' – whether those who invented them were fully aware of the fact or not (I believe they were aware of it, because the Surrealists were always vigorous theoreticians), it is the 'sentences' made with objects which have a meaning and not the single object in itself, in spite of what some people have tried to do or say. The 'ready-made' is an object within a context of objects, and of course, it would be possible to imagine the extreme case of a civilization that was completely imprisoned, as it were, within its technical and material universe, and which would ...

G.C. – would consider it as a work of art?

C.L.-S. ... would, in the end, order it according to several different styles: one or more styles might be utilitarian and scientific, while others would be gratuitous and artistic, the difference between the two depending solely on the arrangement of the elements.

A sea-shell is not the same thing in one of the rooms of the Natural History Museum as it is when in the possession of a curio-collector ... in the same way, certain curves are equations for the mathematician, or marvellous objects.

G.C. Yes, the sculptor exploits the fact.

C.L.-S. But ...

G.C. But I was wondering if it would not be possible to reach a point of coincidence, a point at which the two arrangements coincided absolutely?

C.L.-S. I do not believe that once this course were embarked upon – and I could easily imagine Western civilization going that way – it would be possible to succeed in checking and arresting it at the point you envisage, which would be characterized by a simple and literal redistribution of the elements. The movement would go further and further in the direction of division and recomposition, and where would it end? Perhaps in very detailed figurative painting in which the artist, instead of standing in front of a landscape and giving a more or less transposed and interpreted vision of it, would set about making super-landscapes as Chinese painting has, in fact, always done; it is along these lines that I would expect a solution to the present contradiction to be found : in a kind of synthesis of representativeness, which could once again be carried to extremes, with non-representativeness, which would operate on the level of the free combination of elements.

G.C. Well, I would like to see coincidence between representativeness and non-representativeness in relation to reality, for each individual.

C.L.-S. But I can perfectly well imagine myself being able to live with some large landscape, I can think of one or two examples ... you will perhaps be shocked because I am about to quote minor painters who, curiously enough, as it happens, are now the only ones for whom I still have some feeling: take, for instance, Joseph Vernet's large pictures of the sea-ports of eighteenth-century France which are on display in the main hall of the Musée de la Marine and which are among the few pictures which I always find deeply moving. I can well imagine myself living with these pictures so that the scenes they depict become more real for me than those of real life. For me, their value lies in the fact that they allow me to relive the relationship between sea and land which still existed at that time; a port was a human settlement which did not completely destroy, but rather gave a pattern to, the natural relationships between geology, geography and vegetation, and thus offered an exceptional kind of reality, a dream-world in which we can find refuge.

G.C. In that case, I ought to admit that you are right on all levels, and that I am going off on the wrong tack.

C.L.-S I believe we are both moving in the same direction, but that we do not have exactly the same view of the concrete way in which this orientation or re-orientation of painting ... of the point it might eventually reach. I think it might lead, frankly, to genre painting.

G.C. I would be prepared to envisage the possibility of all art disappearing completely and reality itself being accepted by man as a work of art.

C.L.-S. Oh! man would very quickly get fed up with that situation, since, after all, the combinations we were talking about, the rearrangement of objects in order to bring out their latent properties, are perfectly conceivable but rather limited; after a while, all the possibilities would be exhausted, and I think the best proof of this is the fact that this is not the first time in our history that something of the kind has occurred. Interest in the 'ready-made' (correct me if I am wrong) appeared with Benvenuto Cellini who, in his memoirs, relates how he used to walk along the shore picking up shells and objects carved into shapes by the sea, and how he found inspiration in such things ...

G.C. Yes. In this sense, we can consider other periods in history ...

C.L.-S. In the years preceding the French Revolution, there was also a great vogue for collecting objects. People would buy minerals or shells and give them as presents instead of ornaments. We are again living through a similar period.

G.C. Yes, but the 'ready-made' is not often taken from nature. Nowadays, we use the manufactured object in preference to the natural object.

C.L.-S. Yes, I know, and the manufactured object ...

G.C. There is a preference for scrap-iron rather than ... say, roots.

C.L.-S. Yes, but from this point of view, nature is so much richer than culture; one very quickly exhausts the range of manufactured objects as compared with the fantastic diversity of the animal, vegetable and mineral worlds ... in short, the novel character of the 'ready-made' presents a kind of last resort, before the return to the main source.

G.C. Yes, but it must be remembered that the 'ready-made' we are talking about now is not the same as the one we were talking about a short while ago.

C.L.-S. I agree.

G.C. It is not the same thing at all. When I referred to the generalizing of the function of the 'ready-made', it never occurred to me to limit it to objects manufactured by man, or to such objects when they have been altered by rusting or some other form of damage.

C.L.-S. I quite understand.

G.C. I was thinking of anything that might occur in the natural world.

C.L.-S. Yes, but we would then relapse into an already well-known situation, which has never existed except for very short periods, because man soon gets bored even with what might be called natural art, and begins to yearn again for human art.

VIII

ART AS A SYSTEM OF SIGNS

GEORGES CHARBONNIER. Claude Lévi-Strauss, I would like to ask you a question which is very closely related to one that I have already put. I believe, rightly or wrongly, and I am neither a sociologist nor an anthropologist, that in modern societies such as our own I can detect a break within the group. I mean that, as I see it, part of the group devotes its energies to what might be called, roughly speaking, economic affairs, and another part is concerned with the secretion of culture. I am wondering whether a similar phenomenon is observable in the societies you have studied? Of course, this question overlaps with another – is economic activity an integral part of culture, or not?

CLAUDE LÉVI-STRAUSS. Here again, I think it would be difficult to give you a general reply which would be valid for all the societies studied by anthropologists.

The esoteric nature of culture is evident, it seems to me, in a very great number of societies. You have only to think of priestly castes and guilds of sorcerers to find something analogous to what you were referring to. It is my impression that, as far as our own societies are concerned, the break you mention is due not so much to the fact that these different activities are not carried out by the same individuals as to the absence of personal contact between them. After all, in a native society, the witch-doctor may be a specialist, but he is nevertheless my neighbour. He lives next door, and I know him and meet him every day, and have dealings with him in connection with various secular matters. No doubt I am always conscious of the fact that he is a witch-doctor, and that in his capacity as such he is a repository of supernatural lore, but our relationship is not marked by that strangeness which in Western societies is to be explained essentially by the fact that – to give a crude example – a Renault employee never, or virtually never, has an opportunity of mixing with composers or painters.

G.C. Yes, I quite understand your answer to my question, and I can imagine why you chose this particular example. Only it doesn't correspond exactly to the question as I wanted to put it to you, and which was badly expressed. In the category of the 'Renault employee', I would have liked to put all those people who devote their energies to economic affairs. It is between them and the others that I seem to detect a break.

C.L.-S. Don't you think it can be explained to some extent by the great density and size of contemporary societies, which make it impossible for people with different occupations ever to have an opportunity of meeting each other?

G.C. Yes. I think that even if they knew each other, a certain degree of mistrust would persist. I believe that this mistrust is aroused by certain branches of knowledge – I am careful to say branches in the plural, so that my remarks cannot be taken to apply to scientific knowledge alone. I think that what I have just said is relevant not only to scientific knowledge, but also, perhaps, to 'artistic knowledge'. In short, I think that, generally speaking, the individual who secretes culture, whether he be a scientist, an artist, or an intellectual in any capacity, has no interest for Western society. And not only has it no interest in him, but it mistrusts him; the rest of the nation – or the rest of the group rather – mistrusts him, and it is this fact which leads me to ask you whether the situation is the same in primitive societies.

C.L.-S. It is impossible to find a parallel in societies which, by definition, are extremely different from, and remote from, our own, and which interest us precisely for that reason; we cannot ignore the differences and behave as if they were like us. You are asking the impossible, for your question is almost a contradiction in terms. If, in these societies, we were to find forms of the same type as those existing in Western society ...

G.C. They would be in the same category as Western societies.

C.L.-S. Exactly.

G.C. I quite understand. You think that if there were contact inside our society, this break that I seem to detect would cease to exist?

C.L.-S. Oh, I am not by any means saying that it would cease to exist because – at the risk of appearing to contradict what I was explaining before – in much smaller societies, which consist of a few hundred or a few thousand individuals, and where personal contacts, those that I referred to the other day as authentic relationships, can exist, there are nevertheless divisions which are defined not in terms of esoteric knowledge but in terms of specializations. However, there is no frontier between the two, since a woman who is an excellent potter would only be considered as such because she had certain affinities with the supernatural world, and possessed magical powers which she had inherited, purchased or had had bestowed upon her.

G.C. So – taking, for instance, the sphere of what we call 'art' in the society you are observing, group art is accepted, unreservedly, by everybody.

C.L.-S. Certainly. It is, in fact, closely incorporated into the life of the group. If we try to discover a common language, which would express this difference that you perceive intuitively – and about which I am trying to avoid making any pronouncement, because it is difficult to formulate logically – what is not found in so-called primitive societies, or found only very exceptionally (here again, I am careful not to establish a general rule), is the relationship which is the very basis of our modern conception of artistic activity, that is, the relationship between the creator on the one hand and, on the other, the spectator, or the listener, if the art in question is music. This duality is an exceptional occurrence in primitive societies, because the function of art is probably not the same there. The sign-role of works of art seems to be more prominent in primitive societies; at any rate, it corresponds more exactly to the sociological function assigned to art in such societies.

G.C. And the idea that art is a language does not exist.

C.L.-S. The idea that art is a language can exist in a quite literal sense. We have only to think, first of all, of the various forms of picture-writing which are halfway between writing, that is, language, and a work of art; and then, especially, of the wealth of symbols which can be discerned in the works – I will not say of all so-called primitive communities, but of a great many of them: the North American Indians, for instance, and certain African communities of the Sudan, the Congo or more southerly regions, where each object, even the most utilitarian, is a kind of symbolic concentrate which can be comprehended not only by the creator but by all those who use it.

G.C. Yes. That is far from being the case in our society.

C.L.-S. To take only one very simple example, in certain African communities, it is not customary for husband and wife to take their meals together, and still less so for them to talk while eating; the consumption of food is as private a matter as excretion in our own society; when the wife wants to admonish her husband, she asks a wood-carver to make what, for the sake of brevity, might be called a soup-tureen lid, decorated with symbolic patterns which for the most part refer to popular proverbs – African communities have a great many proverbs. Consequently, the dish itself, the receptacle from which the husband eats his food, is at the same time a message which can be deciphered by the recipient either on his own or with the help of a specialist who has been called in to give advice.

G.C. Yes, so that the distinction we make between 'art' and 'folklore' is out of the question.

C.L.-S. The fact is that artistic innovations are incorporated much more rapidly, indeed almost immediately, into the group culture. All the same, the difference is one of degree rather than of kind. We are inclined to believe that folk art emerges from deep within the collective unconscious, and that the forms in which it manifests itself go back a very long way. This is true in some cases, but not in all. The wheel or rosette designs which can still be observed in rustic furniture, especially in Brittany and the Basque country, date back to a very early period, because they can also be found in several border regions of Europe and even Africa. On the other hand, most of our popular ditties or nursery rhymes, if not all, have not been handed down from a very distant past but more often than not can be traced back to some song or other that was fashionable in eighteenth-century Parisian society and thereafter spread throughout the country and down the social scale from aristocratic and bourgeois circles to the lowest classes of society.

Behind what we call 'popular art' lies something extremely complex – a two-fold movement, which includes on the one hand preservation and, on the other, popularization of themes which were originally upper-class or were considered as such.

G.C. We always come back to the same conclusion: nothing connected with art is foreign to the anthropologist.

C.L.-S. It is impossible, at any rate, for the anthropologist to neglect art in the first place because art is part of culture, and also perhaps for the still more definite reason that art constitutes to the highest degree that take-over of nature by culture which is essentially the type of phenomenon studied by anthropologists.

G.C. This being so, would you say that art is always language, that it amounts to a language?

C.L.-S. Certainly. But not any language. We have already mentioned the craftsmanship aspect which is perhaps the common denominator of all aesthetic manifestations; the fact that, in art, the artist is never completely in control of his materials and technical processes. If he were – and this, I think, is precisely the point which shows why the phenomenon is universal ...

G.C. If he were, art would cease to exist!

C.L.-S. If he were, he would achieve a complete imitation of nature. The model and the work of art would be identical and, consequently, he would be reproducing nature and not creating a specifically cultural object; yet on the other hand, if the problem did not arise, that is if there were no relationship between the work and the source which inspired it, we would find ourselves dealing not with a work of art, but with an object of a linguistic nature. The essential feature of language – as Ferdinand de Saussure so emphatically showed – is that it is a system of signs which have no material relationship with what they are intended to signify. If art were a complete imitation of the object, it would lose its function as sign. We thus arrive, I think, at a conception of art as a signifying system, or a combination of signifying systems, which, however, always remains halfway between language and object.

G.C. It is noticeable that art-critics, in writing their articles, constantly use the word 'language'. Not exactly in the sense you give it, and this is only to be expected, since art critics are not anthropologists. But one gets the impression that the word 'language' has become meaningless.

C.L.-S. Yes, the term 'language', or linguistic terms in general, are often misused. I think that what the art critic or artist really means by 'language' is probably something like 'message', with the implication that the artist is addressing himself to a spectator or a listener. It is this relationship …

G.C. Yes, indeed, it is to avoid the word 'message' that they use 'language'.

C.L.-S. Yes, because 'message' easily takes on mystic overtones – quite wrongly so, as it happens, since the term 'message' is used by communication specialists in a precise and objective way.

G.C. For the artist, it has messianic overtones, and this explains moreover why some artists regard it with distrust.

C.L.-S. Quite. But the use of the term 'language' seems to me, if not dangerous – since we have just affirmed that all art is language – at least often erroneous and indulged in with the purpose of discovering a language or a message where in actual fact they do not exist. Although all art may be language, it is certainly not so at the level of conscious thought; I mean that all the devices at the artist's disposal are so many signs, and that the function of the work of art is to signify an object, to establish a significant relationship with an object.

G.C. This remark prompts me to ask you to define the relationship between art and signification and to state the distinction which should be established between art and language, taking the latter term in the linguistic sense.

C.L.-S. I have to fall back on the distinction I outlined a moment ago – i.e. articulate language is a system of arbitrary signs that have no perceptible relationship with the objects it sets out to signify, whereas, in art, there is some perceptible relationship between the sign and the object.

G.C. Would you make the same assertions in respect of poetry? It seems to me that poetry which uses words and so, to all intents and purposes, appears to function in the linguistic field, can nevertheless claim to have significance outside the realm of linguistics.

C.L.-S. You are right and, in respect of poetry, we must modify the wording of the definition I put forward a moment ago, if not its basic meaning; I said that art is halfway between the object and language; I would now like to say that poetry is halfway between language and art taken in its most general sense. The poet stands in the same relation to language as the painter to the object. Language is his raw material and it is this raw material that he sets out to signify – not exactly the ideas or concepts that we may try to transmit in speech, but those more massive linguistic objects that are constituted by fragments or sections of speech.

G.C. Even if he is misguided about what he is really doing, the poet believes that the conceptual use of the word is a secondary, debased use.

C.L.-S. If you will allow me to use a rather far-fetched comparison, the poet behaves with regard to language like an engineer trying to form heavier atoms from lighter ones; the linguistic objects which the poet creates are weightier than those used in prose; he adds new dimensions to linguistic expression and, in the traditional forms of poetry, the additional demands of rhyme, scansion and all the other rules of prosody are clear to see. Or again, the poet may proceed by a process of disintegration, as Rimbaud does. Poetry therefore seems to exist between two conflicting formulae: linguistic integration and semantic disintegration.

G.C. The two are in operation simultaneously.

C.L.-S. Yes, they are certainly indissolubly linked, but in either case language is considered as an object, and this object is manipulated in such a way as to ensure the addition, or extraction, of some further meaning.

G.C. Yes, but with the paradoxical reservation that the

poet claims, like all artists – although the claim is most obvious in the poet's case – that he is signifying outside the realm of signification, outside the realm of language. According to the poet, the word is something which allows him to use language in order to break away completely from language, and to say more by ceasing totally to signify, – and this, logically, signifies nothing, or so I understand.

C.L.-S. No. Or rather it depends entirely on the meaning you give to the words you are using. If you mean that any form of artistic expression, whether in the plastic arts, poetry or music, aims at the creation of a language which, however, is not, properly speaking, articulate language – indeed, in the case of painting or music, it isn't at all, while in the case of poetry it is quite a different use of articulate language – I think you are absolutely right. If, on the other hand, in the name of the artist, you wanted to claim that signification can exist, over and above any possible or imaginable language, I would say that this is a contradiction in terms.

G.C. I am not unaware of the contradiction in terms. Besides, I wasn't claiming to speak on behalf of the artist, or of anyone else. I think I see such a statement of intention in all the declarations made by artists, whether painters or poets. As regards musicians, the situation may be different. I have never come across a musician who expressed himself in the same way as painters or poets. The musician's vocabulary is different and his claims seem to be different too.

C.L.-S. Yes, but here again, we must make a distinction. We can attribute a certain psychological and subjective attitude to the artist, but after all, the important thing is not what he thinks, but what he does. If this were not so, he would have no need to compose poems or write music or paint pictures. He would quite simply write books.

G.C. Of course.

C.L.-S. So, if you notice that the artists you happen to be acquainted with formulate their aspirations and claims in a manner which is unacceptable, either logically or philosophically, my comment would be: 'This doesn't matter ...'

G.C. I admit that I am forcing the expression of their thoughts to some extent. I have never actually heard artists express themselves so definitely, or state the paradox with such clarity. But I notice that when I develop their statements, I always arrive at this contradiction.

C.L.-S. The important thing is what they do, and not what they believe they are doing.

G.C. Of course.

C.L.-S. And still less the subjective reasons they give

H

themselves. More often than not, in every kind of creation or discovery, the way in which the creator or discoverer first became conscious of it, or first expressed it to himself, is very different indeed from the objective result he obtained.

G.C. Yes. But I think, too, that the artist expresses himself in these terms with a strong desire to reach down into a region or domain beyond the scope of analysis. In the artist's view, his art is distinguished from knowledge by the fact that he thinks himself to be doing something which cannot be the subject of analysis and cannot be gauged in quantitative terms. And this, I think, is his strongest motive.

C.L.-S. Whether he thinks so or not is of no importance, except to the psychologist, and more particularly to the psychologist concerned with aesthetic creation. The real question is: what is he actually doing? Is he, unwittingly and perhaps unwillingly, working out a system of signs which is supplementary to language, or which can exist alongside all the other sign-systems, or – and this seems to me to be much more dangerous – is he saying to us: 'I am working out a new system of signs, I am working out a new code', whereas in fact he is merely working out a pseudo-code? I must confess that this is often the impression I have when I look at abstract, or so-called abstract, painting, since, with regard to it, we can forget the distinction I put forward a moment ago between language and art: abstract painting may present a system of signs, a system which has an intentionally arbitrary relationship with the object. But is the language which is thus imposed upon us willy-nilly a language which is still in contact with the aesthetic emotion, or is it not rather a system of signs like any other, like, say, railway signs, which are different coloured squares or circles conveying various meanings to the engine driver : 'the line is clear', 'the line is blocked', 'a train is coming in the other direction', or 'you must slow down before the level crossing' ... ? But since this is an arbitrary sign-system ...

G.C. Is this certain?

C.L.-S. What do you mean by that?

G.C. It is not certain that these sign-systems are arbitrary : it may not be an accident that green was chosen to mean 'all clear' and red to mean 'halt'.

C.L.-S. You are trying to make me contradict myself, because I once put forward the view that systems like this are not entirely arbitrary. Not that it would have been impossible to use green to signify : 'the track is not clear' and red for the all clear sign, but because the inversion, were it to occur ...

G.C. Would not be an absolute inversion.

C.L.-S. ... would not be an absolute inversion : red would continue to be red, that is, a source of physical

115

and physiological excitement, associated with certain types of reaction which are not entirely arbitrary.

G.C. Incidentally, it seems to me paradoxical to choose red to signify 'stop'.

C.L.-S. Yes, we might in fact ...

G.C. It is more like an incitement to go ahead.

C.L.-S. We could have red as a sign of heat or communicability and green, on the other hand, as a chilling and rather venomous symbol.

G.C. So it might be possible to discover here a deep, underlying meaning, associated ...

C.L.-S. But is this underlying meaning not extremely weak? The apparently arbitrary systems of signals which we use are certainly not as completely arbitrary as they would seem to be in theory. But they are to a very large extent, and much more so than the signs and symbols used by traditional or Cubist painters, or by musicians.

IX

THE DEMANDS OF THE CODE

GEORGES CHARBONNIER. You were saying a moment ago that the abstract painter claims to be detached from the object. This is true. But he certainly does not claim to be detached from nature. On the contrary, he claims to remain close to nature and that it is precisely his detachment from the object which allows him greater significance of statement. Since the object is a hindrance, a barrier, and represents an obligation to give a description and makes rapid synthetizing impossible, the abstract painter will say: 'My abstract picture allows me to make a more rapid and more complete synthesis – if the word 'complete' can be associated with 'synthesis' – than if I were restricted to one object and its recreation.'

CLAUDE LÉVI-STRAUSS. I would, however, not like to give you the impression that my attitude towards abstract painting ...

G.C. Oh, I understand your attitude, and I am merely trying ...

C.L.-S. ... is totally negative. I can be fascinated and charmed by it; it can have a tremendous appeal for me both as colour and form. Nevertheless, when I

look at an abstract picture, I can never decide whether
to hang it on my wall, or whether I would not find
an equally great satisfaction in a piece of driftwood,
or a mineral specimen. Would a sheet of malachite or
a lump of agate not offer me more subtle patterns,
more brilliant and vivid colours for my imagination to
feed on, and to stimulate my mind? In other words,
it is not so much the appeal of abstract painting that
I am questioning, although I would put it in the same
category as the appeal that given objects can have, as
its significance ...

G.C. By specifying clearly ...

C.L.-S. Or rather its signifying character – since significant it obviously is – significant of the painter's intention and of the period when it was painted ...

G.C. Yes! I would even go so far as to say that when
one finds oneself in the presence of an abstract painter,
or of a painter ... for a painter is not necessarily a
man who puts paint on canvas ...

C.L.-S. Yes, but we must not mention names, because
that would involve us in argument!

G.C. There are a few names I can quote. I am thinking,
for instance, of Soulages or Hartung. Well, when I
look at a picture painted by Soulages or Hartung, I get
the impression that I know the whole man. Even his
political opinions. I am considering extreme cases.

Just as I might see, or think I see, from a given Primitive's work, what his angle of approach to society was.

c.l.-s. But don't you think that, in cases such as these, which I accept as being very possible, it is in actual fact because ...

g.c. I think it is possible to discern very clearly in abstract painting that part which consists of completely non-signifying blobs arranged in a purely decorative pattern. Occasionally, in certain pictures, we are aware of a switch to another category. The man himself becomes evident. I am not at all aware of the human element when I look at a painting by Mathieu, for instance. If I look at one of Mathieu's paintings, I learn nothing about Mathieu. If I look at one of Soulages's pictures, I know at once what sort of man Soulages is. In the one instance, the painting has become the poetic expression of the man, in the other, it never reaches this stage at all. (I admit that the artist may have deliberately avoided aiming at it.)

c.l.-s. Yes, but don't you think that, in cases of this kind, what happens is that the painter, while believing himself to be remaining faithful to his formula, has in fact betrayed it, so that, in spite of himself as it were, significant relationships, relationships with the object, have been surreptitiously reintroduced?

g.c. I can see quite clearly that this may be the case. But I am not convinced it is so.

C.L.-S. I would prefer to take an example from music. We find a rather similar situation in music but one which seems to me easier to discuss, because to my knowledge no abstract painter – but you are better acquainted with these matters than I am – has so far put forward a system, or evolved a code. It seems to me that each painter tries to work out his own code and to modify it as he goes along, as he moves from one picture to the next, whereas serial music presents us with a conscious and systematic attempt to provide a new musical grammar, which is intended to replace the traditional grammar.

G.C. Yes, but it is not so very far removed from the traditional grammar.

C.L.-S. To my mind, it is primarily a grammar which operates only as prosody. The rules are poetic, not linguistic ones, since the essential feature of linguistic rules, the feature which makes it possible to express different meanings by means of sounds which in themselves are arbitrary, is that these sounds are part of a system of binary oppositions; in other words, a logical hierarchy is established within the articulatory values which allow us to distinguish between the various meanings.

Now I cannot see at all clearly how the serial code could succeed in maintaining, or rediscovering, a hierarchical system such as this. The idea of opposites remains, but the positions of the notes are not articulated as a system. In this sense, the code would seem to be more expressive than semantic. However, this having been said, when we listen to a work such as *Wozzeck*, which is dodecaphonic rather than purely serial, we feel we are listening to a kind of music that is not at all disconcerting. But is this not because the semantic system of traditional music, the system which finds expression in the hierarchy of notes within the scale and specifies their functions as the leading note, the key-note and the dominant note, has an equivalent here, in spite of the musician's intentions and without his having had any clear conception of what has happened?

G.C. How do these ideas affect your view of *musique concrète*?

C.L.-S. *Musique concrète* seems to me to be very close to the kind of abstract painting we were discussing a moment ago; both are a combination of elements arrived at through the personal likes and dislikes of the painter or composer, but independent of any semantic rule. By chance, a certain kind of meaning may possibly emerge, just as, by chance we may suddenly discover meaning in a natural object, a pebble or a twisted piece of bark, and 'recognize' a flower or a beast (but, when I say 'a meaning', I am not suggesting a resemblance to anything specific, in the way a root may resemble a dragon ...)

G.C. Of course.

C.L.-S. It is simply that we have a sudden vision of the object as a structure and the recognition of the structure in the object gives us an aesthetic emotion, which is purely an effect of chance. And this may happen without any deliberate intention on the part of the artist, without his having been in any real sense instrumental in bringing it about.

G.C. I do not think composers of *musique concrète* would accept these terms.

C.L.-S. Oh, I'm quite sure they wouldn't!

G.C. But I think a number of listeners would reject them too. I can listen to a piece of *musique concrète* and be moved by it. I can even listen to it and give it some kind of form in space. It projects itself in quite a different way from a Beethoven symphony. To my mind, it projects itself more spontaneously into space. If I listen to Philipot's music, for instance, it hasn't at all same meaning, in space, as the music of Beethoven or Mozart.

C.L.-S. The great danger threatening art seems to me to be two-fold. First, instead of being a language, it may become a pseudo-language, a caricature of language, a sham, a kind of childish game on the theme of language, which does not succeed in achieving signification. Secondly, it may become a total language, of the same type as articulate language except for the material it uses, and in this case, it may in all proba-

bility signify but it cannot at the same time be accompanied by any real aesthetic emotion.

What strikes me in your last remarks is that you
make a distinction between *musique concrète* and
Beethoven's music, or the music composed by any
classical or romantic composer, and you say that they
do not provide you with the same experience and
that in one case you organize perception in space; but
is the possibility of organizing perception in space –
which I do not for a moment doubt – accompanied
by aesthetic emotion?

G.C. Yes, if the form of my perception coincides with
something which existed already within me. When I
hear Philipot's music, something very strange happens: I have the impression that I am rediscovering
modes of perception which are peculiar to me. On
listening to Philipot's music, I have the impression
that the composer is telling me how my faculty of
perception operates ...

C.L.-S. In this case, then, I think the conditions of
aesthetic experience are fulfilled, since it seems to me
that what we call aesthetic emotion is linked – or
rather, is the way in which we react when a non-
significant object is promoted to the role of signifier.
As a matter of fact, the point was first made a long
time ago when Boileau wrote: 'There is neither ser-
pent nor odious monster, which when imitated by
art ... ', he was using a poor example, but the true
function of aesthetic transposition or promotion

is to raise to the level of the significant something which did not exist in this mode or form in its raw state.

G.C. Do you look upon the artist as someone who aspires to language?

C.L.-S. He is someone who 'aspires' the object into language (that is breathes it in), if you will allow me to use this expression. He finds himself faced with an object and what actually occurs as he looks at the object is a process of extraction or aspiration which turns the object from a natural into a cultural entity. It is in this sense that, as I said a moment ago, the typical phenomenon which interests the anthropologist, i.e. the relationship between nature and culture and the transition from one to the other, is particularly well exemplified in art.

G.C. Yes. Or rather what you have just defined is not the process as the artist himself sees it. In very many cases the artist thinks, on the contrary, that he is starting from the signifier in order to proceed in a backward or reverse direction.

The artist believes, rather, that he is leaving culture behind and moving towards nature. I am not saying that this is what he does; I am saying that this is what he is trying to do. In the field of art, what is called culture is something which has been made by people who were in fact doing their best to abandon culture and to go back to nature. It is the poet's intention to move in this direction – I repeat, his intention. What is perhaps his real procedure he pejoratively refers to as literature.

C.L.-S. The two things are not contradictory to the extent that the promotion of an object to the rank of sign, if it is successful, must bring out certain fundamental properties which are common both to the sign and the object, i.e. a structure which is evident in the sign and which is normally latent in the object, but which suddenly emerges thanks to its plastic or poetic representation, and which furthermore allows a transition to be made to all sorts of different objects. Consequently, I agree with you. There is a two-fold movement: an aspiration of nature towards culture, that is of the object towards the sign and towards language, and a second movement which, through such linguistic expression, allows us to discover or perceive properties of the object which are normally concealed and which are the very properties it has in common with the structure and functioning of the human mind.

G.C. I think we can say that art is achieved only if the second movement occurs.

C.L.-S. Certainly.

G.C. There is surely no achievement of art before it occurs. You are therefore disinclined to consider abstract painting as a form of artistic expression?

C.L.-S. I can only give you a very subjective reply, but after all ... I would be a very bad anthropologist if, during the present discussion, I did not constantly bear in mind that you and I, alas, do not belong to the same generation, and that I learnt to look and feel on the basis of quite different models from those you have always been accustomed to. In endeavouring to produce a rational justification for – I will not say my antipathy but rather my indifference – to abstract painting, I may not be putting forward sound arguments based on reason, but attempting to rationalize an historical attitude, which is that of certain individuals of my generation and social environment when they find themselves faced with something which did not exist when they were adolescents.

G.C. Your argument could not apply to me because I am not young enough to have seen nothing but abstract painting.

C.L.-S. But it was abstract painting which gave you an opportunity to make a stand against your contemporaries, or against the generation immediately preceding yours ...

G.C. That is undoubtedly the case.

C.L.-S. And I am quite sure that my adolescent passion for Cubism is to be explained not only by a straightforward and genuine relationship between myself and the pictures I was looking at, but also by the fact that it gave me an opportunity to break away from my elders and to take a stand against them.

G.C. Yes, I know that people always talk about taking a stand 'against' something or other. I am not happy about the expression, because the aim is not so much opposition as something else. At any rate, it is not quite the same thing as opposition.

C.L.-S. We were talking about the relationship between art and language. You know the anecdote that Bergson quotes, about a peasant woman who went to church while on a visit to a remote village and was the only person not to laugh at a joke made by the priest in his sermon. On being asked why she did not laugh, she replied, 'I do not belong to the parish.' In all language phenomena, there is more than just communication : there is also an attempt to work out modes of communication which are peculiar to a particular group, or generation, or social environment.

G.C. I know villages in the Cotentin where the most common words are used with meanings different from their normal or accepted senses. I know villages – I cannot tell you their names, through fear of offending the inhabitants – where taciturn, for instance, means gay, and where the majority of words are used in this way, so that the local speech is literally incomprehensible.

C.L.-S. Yes, but this explains why we cannot leave the

group out of account when we are trying to understand our preference for such and such a mode of artistic expression.

G.C. I was saying a moment ago that the poet, although he considers himself as operating in the field of linguistics, aims at avoiding signification through a special use of words. Do you as a philosopher consider this to be a philosophical attitude or not?

C.L.-S. When I think of poetry and the creative processes peculiar to it, it is not philosophical or metaphysical images or considerations which spring to mind. I tend rather to visualize the poet as a chemist trying to produce large molecules synthetically: he is trying to create large linguistic entities, compact objects, the basic substance of which is linguistic in nature: he is aiming at a kind of meta-language, if you like, provided the prefix 'meta' is not given any metaphysical connotation.

G.C. Can what you have just said be applied to painting? Might it be possible, by transposing all the terms, to maintain that the abstract painter operates like this? Is he, in his own way, looking for large molecules in the world of forms and colours?

C.L.-S. No, there is an immense difference. The materials which the poet uses are already endowed with signification. They are words or groups of words which have meanings and, by combining them, the

128

poet tries to vary, change or enrich these meanings, whereas the materials used by an abstract painter, i.e. touches of paint, from the moment they cease to have any explicit relationship with reality are not elements which have any meaning in themselves. You may retort that the same thing applies to language, and the same thing does in fact apply, since the constituent elements of speech which linguists call phonemes ...

G.C. Have no link with meaning ...

C.L.-S. No affinity with meaning. For instance, *p* and *t* have no intrinsic meaning in French yet they are used to distinguish the two meanings associated with the words '*pas*' and '*tas*'. You may say that the same thing applies to painting: the spot of paint on the canvas has no intrinsic significance, but can be used to distinguish between shades of significance. To which I would reply that this could be true of a painting which had some relationship, however remote, with an object, and in which the touch of paint could be used, for instance, to distinguish between form and content, contours and colours, light and shadow, and so on ... but not in a system in which the touch of paint represents the sum total of that system and there is no second code *over and above the touch of paint itself*, and the painter considers that he has the right to formulate his rules on a single level.

G.C. But in this case, the procedure of the abstract artist cannot be developed indefinitely. To pursue it is another way of getting back to decoration and staying there.

C.L.-S. For my part, this is how I react to abstract painting; it can have certain charms for me but I cannot get away from its decorative aspect. In my view it lacks the essential attribute of the work of art, which is to offer a kind of reality of a semantic nature.

G.C. If I think about abstract painting, I cannot consider it as a gratuitous phenomenon. Even if I were able to determine the exact moment when it came into being, the precise instance when it appeared for the first time – supposing it were possible to do so – the fact nevertheless remains that abstract painting takes its place in an uninterrupted tradition of painting.

C.L.-S. That is undeniable.

G.C. We are therefore led to believe that, by the mere fact of its existence, it corresponds to an internal law of that historical movement which we can refer to as painting. Looking at it from this angle, I cannot condemn abstract painting absolutely and am inclined to think that it follows on naturally from the work of Raphael and Michelangelo.

C.L.-S. I would agree with you on that point. But the essential problem is to know whether, for the past few centuries, the evolution of pictorial art has been a constructive advance, or whether it has been progressively destructive, so that, at this moment, we may be experiencing the last phase of the destruction.

X

THE FUTURE OF PAINTING

CLAUDE LÉVI-STRAUSS. After all – and at this point I can speak again as an anthropologist – painting is not an inevitable feature of culture: a society can perfectly well exist without any form of pictorial art. So, it is not inconceivable that after abstract art ...

GEORGES CHARBONNIER. There may be no more painting?

C.L.-S. Yes. A kind of total detachment, heralding the advent of an 'a-pictorial' era.

G.C. I know some painters who think so, but not all share this view. The painters who think along these lines are for the most part very young. And since they are very young, this is precisely why their judgment is less acceptable, because we have no idea to what extent they are guilty of 'laziness' in their approach to nature.

C.L.-S. In any case, we cannot depend on opinions. They are collective phenomena which lie beyond verification. We have no idea what is going to happen to painting in the future, and I don't think it is possible to make any forecast: there may be a kind of disruption or disintegration of pictorial art before it finally disappears, or a new beginning which is being prepared for in the sort of Middle Ages through which we are now living. And I am using the term 'Middle Ages' not in any pejorative sense but because I seem to see a resemblance between certain aspects of the researches and speculations of abstract painters and certain modes of medieval thought: notably the striving towards a gnosis, i.e. towards a form of knowledge which might transcend science or towards a language which would be a para-language.

G.C. Yes, but what you have just said is characteristic of any art.

C.L.-S. Depending on the period, art adopts an attitude of greater or lesser hostility towards the external world. For Renaissance artists, painting was perhaps an instrument of knowledge but it was also an instrument of possession, and we must not forget, when we are dealing with Renaissance painting, that it was only possible because of the immense fortunes which were being amassed in Florence and elsewhere, and that rich Italian merchants looked upon painters as agents, who allowed them to confirm their possession of all that was beautiful and desirable in the world. The pictures in a Florentine palace represented a kind of microcosm in which the proprietor, thanks to his artists, had recreated within easy reach and in as real a form as possible, all those features of the world to which he was attached.

G.C. I believe that a man like Max Ernst – I don't think I am misrepresenting his attitude – would say that the reason why abstract painting, on the other hand, has so many devotees at the present time, and devotees who naturally also belong to the wealthiest class, is that abstract painting – and here I am going against all I said a moment ago – raises no issues. This, in fact, is the major charge he levels against it. Max Ernst condemns abstract painting precisely because, in his view, it does not signify. But now I am arguing on your side ...

C.L.-S. But perhaps not along the lines I indicated a moment ago.

G.C. No, not along the same lines.

C.L.-S. However, you are certainly not contradicting my argument.

G.C. He says one has only to look at the countries which buy abstract painting. They are precisely those countries where people are not given to self-questioning and even want to eliminate all self-questioning in favour of concentration on business. So they buy abstract art because it is reassuring, and because, should they happen to look up from their desks, their peace of mind is not disturbed by any kind of religious or social problem. It causes no uneasiness and is even reassuring. Faced with abstract painting, they are self-confident and their consciences are clear. This is a point of view I personally cannot accept, at least not completely; I cannot accept it in such a crude form.

C.L.-S. Leaving aside the basis of the argument, we may accept the fact that the role of art in society – in every society, I should say, because for once I am ready to generalize – is not simply to provide the consumer (let us refer to him as such) with a sensuous satisfaction. Art is also a guide, a means of instruction, I might almost say a way of acquiring knowledge of reality. I have already stressed the fact (but I refer to it again because I believe it to be important) that Impressionist painting does not merely imply a transformation or revolution in pictorial technique and in a new way of looking at things. It also brought about a revolution in the subject-matter of painting, which we have already defined as follows: classical, and even romantic, painters were interested only in noble and grandiose landscapes. They needed mountains, majestic trees, etc., whereas Impressionism was satisfied with far less – a field, cottages and a few spindly trees ... And the unpretentiousness of subject-matter cannot be dissociated from the Impressionist painter's interest in the transitory aspect of things, which is the temporal aspect of what I have just pointed out in the spatial context.

G.C. Yes. In theory every series of canvasses had the same purpose.

C.L.-S. That is so. Therefore, however much we may admire the Impressionists, we would hardly seem to be maligning them in saying that, in the last resort, their painting is that of a society which is realizing that it must give up a great many things which were still accessible to previous periods. The ennoblement and aesthetic promotion of suburban landscapes can be explained perhaps by the fact that they, too, are beautiful, although this had previously not been recognized, but it is mainly a consequence of the fact that the great landscapes which had inspired Poussin were no longer available to the same extent to the people of the nineteenth century. Soon they will have completely ceased to exist. Civilization is destroying them more or less everywhere, and mankind must learn to make do with more modest delights.

G.C. Yes. The same amount of beauty has to be projected on to things which, in themselves, are not beautiful.

C.L.-S. Yes. It is a sign that the world is in the process of changing, and it seems to me that the upheaval we observe in the case of Impressionism, when we compare it with previous art forms, can be seen once more in the case of Cubism, which undertakes to teach men to live on friendly terms not so much with restricted suburban landscapes (for Montmartre was already bristling with dismal-looking buildings) as with the products of human industry. The world in which twentieth century man has to live no longer admits even of those relatively rustic spots dear to Sisley or Pissarro. It is a world completely invaded by culture and the products of culture, and so develops a form of painting which seeks its chief sources of inspiration in manufactured objects.

G.C. In this sense, abstract painting can be completely justified. If I admit that the abstract painter says the manufactured object is beautiful, but that it already belongs to the past and that now everything is in fact ugly and that, consequently, I cannot even find an object worthy of the amount of beauty I can project ...

C.L.-S. But in that case you will be forced to agree that there is a relationship of complementarity between abstract painting and the painting – *horribile dictu* – of an artist like Bernard Buffet. It is as if the latter were saying to us: 'Everything is ugly. I am showing you things as being even uglier than they are, because you must get used to living with ugliness, because it is all you have left', while the abstract painter declares: 'I am resolutely turning my back on all these things and I am painting, but what am I painting?'

G.C. Purely and simply, that inner beauty which I

would like to bestow on objects and can no longer bestow on them.

C.L.-S. But I much prefer to bestow this non-objectivized beauty on certain choice objects, such as shells or pebbles.

G.C. Yes, I quite understand. I was not in any sense attempting to contradict your argument. I was trying to see if I could apply to abstract painting the argument you were putting forward in the case of the Impressionists and Cubists.

C.L.-S. Such as?

G.C. The latter say: 'Be satisfied with what you have,' and the former: 'That's the kind of world you live in.'

C.L.-S. I agree, except that ... the world we live in is not the world of abstract painting. The latter yearns for a kind of escape, and this brings us back to the remarks by Max Ernst which you were quoting a moment ago.

G.C. Admittedly, but why should I deprive myself of painting, if it offers me something I think superior to what the world can offer me?

C.L.-S. That is one solution. I am not convinced that it is the only possible one, or the most likely. As I have said elsewhere, are we not about to witness a complete reversal of this trend, a return to professional painting, to *trompe-l'œil* which will seek inspiration not in the imitation of an external object (because we know now that this is too easy – the technical means at our disposal, and the experience accumulated by painters over the centuries would turn such imitation into a pure question of craftsmanship) but in the re-creation of an objective world to which we shall probably never have access and which we can try to conjure up through painting?

G.C. People can believe anything if they set their minds to it. Might it not be said that man's way of apprehending the world around him is undergoing a change? You were talking about the beauty of landscapes as they were painted a few centuries ago, and about landscapes, the ordered arrangement of nature and palaces, all of which are things of the past. Were man suddenly to decide that what he is looking at is beautiful, it would be so at once. There is no reason why the majesty typical of Poussin's landscapes should not suddenly be transferred to the Parc Monceau. Will this not be necessary if, as you think, there is a possibility of a sudden return to a certain kind of painting, roughly speaking, to the kind defined by Dali? It is obvious that we shall have to be prepared to alter our way of looking at things from one day to the next.

C.L.-S. Not necessarily.

G.C. Majesty, beauty and grandeur will have to be placed in a different context. And ...

C.L.-S. We could perfectly well set ourselves the task of giving a painstaking and extremely literal representation of certain forms of beauty, while at the same time admitting that these forms of beauty no longer exist in the world around us, and have to be invented.

G.C. I have noticed a very curious thing. In talking with friends of mine, I have had occasion to discuss the vast concrete awning which stands on its three corners in the Place de la Défense. What strikes me is that very few people – I can even say that I have found none at all – have the courage to say openly that it is 'beautiful' or 'ugly'. 'Extraordinary' is their verdict. One can sense their amazement, and it is an amazement bordering on admiration; then, after a movement of revulsion which prompts the criticism that it is like a station entrance hall, vaguely reminiscent at the same time of an eighteenth-century house, they add an 'And yet ... ', which indicates a swing back to admiration. They wonder if it may not be one of the architectural forms of the future, and have not yet made up their minds. If people were suddenly to decide that it was beautiful, it would be so, and all Poussin's majesty would be transferred to the vast concrete awning ...

C.L.-S. First of all, it may be neither beautiful nor ugly,

but belong to a different category altogether. Not everything is to be defined in relation to beauty or ugliness. Things can also belong to a type of beauty which is not exactly the kind we would call aesthetic. I have always appreciated the beauty of big, modern cities, particularly New York, but New York does not strike me as being beautiful like a work of art, nor even a man-made object; but rather like a landscape, which is the contingent product of thousands of years.

G.C. You say: 'It strikes me as being beautiful in the way a landscape is beautiful.' This links New York with nature and not with culture.

C.L.-S. Yes, and I mean by that that the Palais du Rond-Point de la Défense can seem beautiful to us, but in the way a mountain is beautiful and not like a monument.

G.C. Is this not a phenomenon peculiar to our day and age? Is man not beginning to produce things which have more resemblance to nature than to culture? Might there not be some fundamental change taking place in works of art so that, instead of reflecting nature or rediscovering it, they 'add' to it?

C.L.-S. What you have defined there is a characteristic feature not so much of the aesthetic activity of modern man as of his scientific and technical activities. All the great creations of modern science bring man into increasingly direct contact with nature, adapt him to it and turn him into a kind of instrument or agent for the demonstration of the great natural laws; some such laws, which have no observable manifestation in given nature, have disclosed their existence through the works of man, as is the case with the use of nuclear power for either peaceable or war-like purposes ...

G.C. Man secretes nature by adding to the consequences of its laws, if not by adding new laws.

C.L.-S. Yes, but will society achieve aesthetic satisfaction in so doing? Or will it not transpose such satisfaction into a different sphere?

G.C. The phenomenon is so new that the artist too will have something to say about it. It is the essential phenomenon.

C.L.-S. You know, I am not so sure of that, because if we look for guidance to the example of primitive societies which are obviously far removed from our own as regards power over nature, we see that, precisely because they are handicapped, these societies are also in a sense directly linked with nature, through deficiency rather than through excess, because they are without the means to free themselves from certain determined natural processes. Yet these societies have located their aesthetic expression and found aesthetic satisfaction in all kinds of relationships with the supernatural: their art is magical or religious. It follows that the connection does not seem to me to be in any sense necessary, and there again, we are dealing with a mode of adaptation that we are hardly in a position to foresee.

G.C. I believe that, at the present time, the artist is already very conscious of what you were saying a moment ago when you were talking about laws of which previously there was no observable manifestation. When man gives these laws which exist – they had not been formulated but were potentially definable since they have been formulated subsequently – when man gives these laws an opportunity to operate, he is certainly adding nature to nature. He is gilding the lily, as it were. And the artist sees this, or at least he is vaguely conscious of it. He will incorporate this consciousness, however vague, however obscure, into his researches.

C.L.-S. I don't think this will produce a form of art I shall like!

G.C. I wonder if, for the artist, abstract painting is not a way of allowing laws of which there has been no observable manifestation to disclose their existence, and if the characteristic feature of modern art is not, in the first place, an ability to add to that which already exists a determination to bring into being those potentialities which are the consequence of what is? Of course, I have no intention of introducing a supernatural element into this extension of nature ...

C.L.-S. Don't you think it would be a mistake to consider art exclusively in relation to the outside world and nature, instead of thinking of it in relation to its own world, which is the world of art itself? I am less aware of the relationships between the artist and the outside world than of those between a particular artist and the other artists who preceded him in time. There is an 'order' of painting, a kind of closed world, and it seems to me that the painter of today is reacting much more in relationship to the painters of the past than he is to the world of today.

G.C. Have we not to conclude that everyone is moving more or less in the same direction? That all human movements are more or less concomitant, more or less interlinked?

C.L.-S. Links there most certainly are. I am not maintaining that everything happens with total arbitrariness, and that civilizations are made up of bits and pieces.

G.C. Twelve-tone music did not appear at the same time as Van Eyck's painting. It seems to me to be more closely linked to the tensions of urban industrialized society than to the use of chromatism.

C.L.-S. I must confess that I don't see the connection. It seems much easier to me to try to understand the case of twelve-tone music in relation to the musical forms which immediately preceded it, than in relation to the whole society in which it is now occurring.

G.C. There must, nevertheless, be a link between the state of music and the society in which it occurs. Even if I am unable to define it.

C.L.-S. Naturally, there must be one.

G.C. The concomitance of phenomena cannot be 'haphazard'. I was about to say 'must have a meaning', but I realize that it would be wrong to use such terms in this context.

C.L.-S. Yes, but you must constantly keep both aspects in mind. In each category, there are delays and accelerations. I have a feeling, for instance, that music has always been much more 'avant-garde' than other forms of aesthetic expression: the music composed at the time of the Impressionist movement was much more adventurous musically than Impressionism was pictorially.

G.C. Did it not have a somewhat similar approach to sensation?

C.L.-S. Only to a very slight extent, I would say.

G.C. There is a rather similar phenomenon of 'decomposition', I think, in Impressionist painting and in the music composed at the time of the Impressionist movement.

C.L.-S. Let us say that to us modern listeners, it does not appear so dated!

K

XI

CULTURE AND LANGUAGE

GEORGES CHARBONNIER. Claude Lévi-Strauss, we have now come to the last conversation of this series. Not being an anthropologist myself, I have tried, in pursuing our dialogue, to give you the part of the anthropologist, or scientist. This is why I have asked the kind of questions which would oblige you as an anthropologist to overstep the boundaries of your speciality, but less, indeed far less, than might at first appear, since I have borne in mind that the anthropologist who appeals to mathematics to help him, also appeals to poetic apprehension. He is perhaps the only scientist who needs to aim at identification with his subject, with the 'other'. He has also – in extending his knowledge – to discover the poetic properties of language. When I imagine I am luring the anthropologist beyond his field of study, or pretend to be doing so, I am well aware that I am asking him to have recourse to poetic apprehension. But the questions I am asking the scientist are not the same as the questions he asks himself, and we are anxious to know what kind of questions he puts to himself; with the usual rider, of course, that we ordinary men in the street are – with undoubted naivety – asking for instruction from the expert. We would like to know

what conclusion he has reached, since we want con-
clusions; what message he has for us, since we mean
him to communicate with us; and what he has to say
to other scientists, since we hope that, through him,
because he is a poet as well as a scientist, the
human element will be preserved. So I would like to
put one last question to you. We ordinary men in the
street talk – in very vague terms – about nature and
culture. You, as a scientist, talk about nature and
culture using a precise terminology. What distinction is it appropriate to make between nature and
culture?

CLAUDE LÉVI-STRAUSS. For the anthropologist this is
the fundamental distinction and one which presents
certain difficulties for French anthropologists, because
the term 'culture', which is a borrowing from English,
hasn't the same traditional meaning in French as was
given to it by the founders of the anthropological
sciences. Nature is everything in our make-up that we
owe to biological heredity; culture, on the other
hand, is what we receive from external tradition and,
to refer to Tylor's classic definition – I am quoting
from memory and no doubt inaccurately – culture, or
civilization, is the sum total of the customs, beliefs,
and institutions such as art, law, religion, and techniques for dealing with the material world, in short,
all the habits or skills learnt by man as a member of
a community. There are, therefore, two major cate-
gories of facts: one links us to the animal kingdom
by virtue of everything we are, because of our birth

and the characteristics which have been passed down to us by our parents and ancestors, these characteristics being of a biological, and sometimes of a psychological, nature; the other consists of the whole artificial universe which we live in as members of a community. Anthropology[1] endeavours, in the realm of culture, to carry out the same task of description, observation, classification and interpretation that the zoologist or botanist accomplishes in the realm of nature. It is, incidentally, in this sense that anthropology can be said to be a natural science, or that it aspires to establish itself as a science on the level of the other natural sciences.

G.C. In a sense, then, culture must originate in nature?

C.L.-S. Let us say that it implies a number of factors which belong to the realm of nature. It is indisputable that, in any and every society, men have the same basic needs: they have to procure food, protect themselves against the cold, breed, and so on.

G.C. But how is culture evolved?

C.L.-S. These needs are identical throughout the human species precisely in so far as they are basic and natural in origin. What interests the anthropologist and what belongs to the realm of culture, is the different modulations, if I may use the word, undergone in various societies and at various times, by the basic

[1] 'L'ethnologie ou, au sens large, l'anthropologie, essaie de faire ... (etc.)'

148

material, which is by definition always and everywhere identical.

G.C. What is the sign which is taken as being indica-
tive of culture? The most elementary sign?

C.L.-S. For a very long time it was considered to be –
and many anthropologists may still be of this opinion
– the presence of manufactured objects. Man has been
described as *homo faber*, the maker of tools, and this
characteristic has been accepted as the essential mark
of culture. I confess that I do not agree, and that one
of my essential aims has always been to establish the
line of demarcation between culture and nature, not
in tool-making, but in articulate speech. It is with
language that the leap forward occurs; suppose we
were to find living beings who made tools, on some
unknown planet; we could not deduce from this fact
alone that they belonged to the human category.
Actually, we find such creatures on our own planet,
since certain animals are capable, up to a point, of
making tools or objects approximating to tools. Yet we
do not consider that they have accomplished the
transition from nature to culture. But imagine that
we came across living beings who had a language,
however different from our own, which was translatable into our own language, and who were therefore
beings with whom we could communicate ...

G.C. A language consisting of signs or words – any kind
of language?

C.L.-S. Any imaginable kind of language, since the essential feature of a language is that it should be translatable. Otherwise it would not be a language because it would not be a system of signs necessarily capable of conversion into another sign-system by a process of transformation. Ants can construct extraordinarily complicated underground palaces, and indulge in such sophisticated forms of cultivation as the growing of mushrooms, which, at one particular stage of development – not a stage that occurs spontaneously in nature – are suitable as food for ants, yet for all that ants belong to the animal kingdom. But if we could exchange messages with them and engage in discussions with them, the situation would be quite different; this would be a cultural, not a natural, phenomenon.

G.C. So all problems relate to language?

C.L.-S. I think all problems are linguistic ones, as we were saying in connection with art. Language seems to me to be the cultural phenomenon *par excellence*, for several reasons. First of all, because language is part of culture, one of the skills or habits we acquire from external tradition; secondly, because language is the essential instrument, the special means by which we assimilate group culture ... a child acquires its culture because people talk to it; it is scolded or encouraged by means of words; lastly, and most important of all, because language is the most perfect of all those cultural manifestations which, in one respect or another, constitute systems, and if we want to understand art, religion or law, and perhaps even cooking or the rules of politeness, we must imagine them as being codes formed by articulated signs, following the pattern of linguistic communication.

G.C. May we then suppose that poetry, since it has a more special relationship with language than other forms of art, came into being before them, or did it, on the contrary, occur later?

C.L.-S. I don't see any need to establish such a connection. The use of language for poetic purposes might even be more difficult and more complex than other aesthetic forms, since the latter use and combine raw materials in a linguistic mode, whereas poetry performs a secondary operation with materials provided by language itself.

G.C. Language is therefore the definition of culture, the essential feature of culture. All problems are problems of language. But are not all problems fundamentally problems of nature?

C.L.-S That depends on the kind of problem you have in mind.

G.C. Is every problem not connected ultimately with the study of some aspect of nature?

C.L.-S. Here again, it is a question of definition. If by

nature you understand all the manifestations of the world in which we live, there is no doubt about culture itself being a part of nature. When we contrast nature and culture, we are taking the term nature in a more restricted sense to refer to those features in man which are transmitted through biological heredity. From this point of view, nature and culture are opposites, since culture derives not from biological heredity but from external tradition – that is from education. Now you may say: culture itself, the fact that men exist, use language and have become organized into societies which differ from each other in their customs and institutions – you may say that all this, from a certain point of view, is part of nature, and you are entitled to assume – although the assumption would be a metaphysical one – that nature is a unified and homogeneous whole. From the practical point of view there is no need to do this, since, at least for the time being, science offers us what might be called a 'laminated' representation of nature, in which discontinuities appear between the layers, with the result that the discontinuity between nature and culture, in the anthropological sense, may be only one form of discontinuity, among many others: the form which allows us, in practice, to define the limits of our field of study.

G.C. Is this discontinuity due to nature or to language?

C.L.-S. From a methodological point of view, language is not a phenomenon of nature.

G.C. But I can only study nature by means of language.

C.L.-S. No doubt: and science itself which studies nature is a phenomenon of culture.

G.C. So, when I discover discontinuity, how can I be sure that it is in nature and not in the instrument with which I am studying it?

C.L.-S. You are raising very large questions, philosophical questions, which philosophers would undoubtedly consider to be both very important and very interesting. But if the anthropologist allowed himself to be obsessed by problems of this kind, he would become a philosopher and cease to practise anthropology. His function is a more modest one. It consists in marking out a particular sector, which is the total category of cultural phenomena, and within this prescribed field the anthropologist undertakes a task which is comparable to that performed by the botanist, the zoologist or the entomologist, a task of description and classification ... Of course, this does not mean that we do not, in our leisure moments, consider such major problems (even if we wanted to, we could not avoid thinking about them), but they lie beyond the scope of anthropologist. If what I was saying a moment ago is true, namely that the criterion of culture is language, the problem you are posing takes us back to the problem of the origin of language. You know that this is an outstandingly controversial issue and that for a very long time now philosophers have been struggling with the contradictory fact that language has not always existed but that, on the other hand, no one understands how it came into being, since it was not enough, for it to come into being, that someone should invent speech – the person who was being addressed had to understand what was being said to him. If and when we solve the problem of the origin of language, we shall understand how culture can appear within nature and how the transition from one category to the other was able to occur. But the problem is not an anthropological one; it is concerned with the fundamental difference between man's intellectual processes and those of the animals, with the structure of the human brain, and the emergence of a specifically human function, the use of symbols ... This is a psychological problem and even an anatomical and a physiological one, in so far as it will necessarily entail the clarification of the structure and working of the brain; it is, I imagine, a problem, the solution of which may be quite considerably speeded up by cybernetics, and by electronic calculating machines which make it possible to study experimentally the level of complexity that certain forms of activity – which resemble cerebral activity to a certain extent – can objectively correspond to. But this is no longer an anthropological problem. All the anthropologist can do is say to his colleagues in other branches of study that the real question is the question of language. If you solve the problem of the nature and origin of language, we can explain the rest : what culture is, and how it made its appearance;

what art is and what technological skills, law, philosophy and religion are. But it is not within the scope
of us anthropologists to rend the veil. All we know
is that all the peoples of the world, all mankind in its
most ancient and humble manifestations, has been
endowed with articulate speech, that the emergence
of language coincides exactly with the emergence of
culture and that, for this very reason, the solution
cannot be provided by anthropologists. We start off
with language as a given element.

SELECTED BIBLIOGRAPHIES

A list of the principal works of Claude Lévi-Strauss,
with the dates of their first appearance

LA VIE FAMILIALE ET SOCIALE DES INDIENS NAMBIKWARA
(Société des Américanistes, Paris, 1948)

LES STRUCTURES ÉLÉMENTAIRES DE LA PARENTÉ (Presses
Universitaires de France, 1949), translated as THE
ELEMENTARY STRUCTURES OF KINSHIP (Eyre & Spot-
tiswoode, London, 1969)

'INTRODUCTION À L'ŒUVRE DE MARCEL MAUSS', in M.
Mauss, SOCIOLOGIE ET ANTHROPOLOGIE (P.U.F., 1950)

RACE ET HISTOIRE (UNESCO, 1952), translated as RACE
AND HISTORY (UNESCO, 1952)

TRISTES TROPIQUES (Plon, 1958), translated as WORLD
ON THE WANE (Hutchinson, 1961)

ANTHROPOLOGIE STRUCTURALE (Plon, 1958), translated
as STRUCTURAL ANTHROPOLOGY (Basic Books, New
York, 1963)

'LA GESTE D'ASDIWAL' (ANNUAIRE DE L'ÉCOLE PRATIQUE
DES HAUTES ÉTUDES, 5ième Section, 1958–9, 1960),
translated as 'THE STORY OF ASDIWAL', in E. Leach
(editor), THE STRUCTURAL STUDY OF MYTH AND
TOTEMISM (Tavistock Publications, 1967)

ENTRETIENS AVEC CLAUDE LÉVI-STRAUSS (with Georges
Charbonnier), (Plon-Julliard, 1961)

LE TOTÉMISME AUJOURD'HUI (P.U.F., 1962), translated as
TOTEMISM (Merlin Press, 1964)

LA PENSÉE SAUVAGE (Plon, 1962), translated as THE SAVAGE MIND (Weidenfeld & Nicolson, 1966)
MYTHOLOGIQUES : LE CRU ET LE CUIT (Plon, 1964)
MYTHOLOGIQUES : DU MIEL AUX CENDRES (Plon, 1966)
MYTHOLOGIQUES : L'ORIGINE DES MANIÈRES DE TABLE (Plon, 1968)

A list of the principal works of Georges Charbonnier, with the dates of their first appearance

GUSTAVE SINGIER (Georges Fall, Paris, 1958)
ENTRETIENS AVEC ANDRÉ MASSON (Julliard, Paris, 1958)
ANTONIN ARTAUD (Seghers, Paris, 1959)
MONOLOGUE DU PEINTRE, two volumes (Julliard, Paris, 1960)
ENTRETIENS AVEC RAYMOND QUENEAU (Gallimard, Paris, 1962)
ENTRETIENS AVEC JACQUES AUDIBERTI (Gallimard, Paris, 1965)
ENTRETIENS AVEC JORGE LUIS BORGES (Gallimard, Paris, 1967)
ENTRETIENS AVEC MICHEL BUTOR (Gallimard, Paris, 1967)

CLAUDE LÉVI-STRAUSS

Claude Lévi-Strauss was born in 1908 in Belgium and educated at the University of Paris in Philosophy and Law. From 1935 to 1939 he taught at the University of São Paulo, Brazil, and first came into contact with Amazon Indians. He served in the army in 1939. From 1942 to 1945 he worked at the New School for Social Research and the École Libre des Hautes Études in New York, subsequently becoming Cultural Attaché at the French Embassy from 1946–7. On his return to France in 1947 he became, successively, Associate Director of the Musée de l'Homme, Directeur d'Études at the École Pratique des Hautes Études and the Editor of *L'Homme, revue française d'anthropologie*. He is an Honorary Fellow : Royal Anthropological Institute of Great Britain and Ireland; Foreign Fellow : American Philosophical Society; American Academy of Arts and Sciences; Royal Academy of the Netherlands; Norwegian Academy of Science and Letters; Doctor *honoris causa* : Université Libre de Bruxelles; Yale University; Oxford University; *Officier de la Légion d'Honneur*. Since 1960, Claude Lévi-Strauss has been Professor of Social Anthropology at the Collège de France.

GEORGES CHARBONNIER

Born in Paris, Georges Charbonnier studied Law at the Faculté de Droit and the École Libre des Sciences Politiques in that city. He has been a leading Producer on the French Radio since 1949, specializing in relations between the arts and the sciences. He is now responsible for the programmes 'Sciences et Techniques', 'Le Secret Professionnel' and 'Paris à l'Écoute du Monde' on the equivalent of our Third Programme: France-Culture.

CAPE EDITIONS